Connecting with Our Children

Guiding Principles for Parents in a Troubled World

Roberta Gilbert, M.D.

John Wiley & Sons, Inc.

New York • Chichester • Weinheim • Brisbane • Singapore • Toronto

This book is dedicated to my parents, Robert and Mae Gilbert, who have shown their children what an excellent marriage looks like close up and who have nurtured and encouraged me always in every way possible to be the best I can be.

Contents

Acknowledgments VII

A Personal Foreword I

PART ONE
REARING CHILDREN IN A TROUBLED WORLD

CHAPTER 1   What in the World Is Happening?................. 11

CHAPTER 2   How Problems Develop in Young People 19

CHAPTER 3   Why Johnny Isn't Learning 25

CHAPTER 4   Irresponsible Behavior and Substance Abuse 31

CHAPTER 5   Emotional Illness 37

CHAPTER 6   Physical Illness 43

CHAPTER 7   Family Violence 47

CHAPTER 8   Beyond the Problem Focus...................... 55

PART TWO
HOW SUCCESSFUL PARENTS THINK
—A SYNOPSIS OF BOWEN FAMILY
SYSTEMS THEORY FOR PARENTS

CHAPTER 9   Families Are Systems 61

CHAPTER 10   Anxiety and Its Crucial Effects 71

CHAPTER 11 The Family as an Emotional Unit—
Reactivity in Action. 79

CHAPTER 12 The Wonderful Range of People and Families 91

CHAPTER 13 Why Children in the Same Family
Turn Out So Differently 103

CHAPTER 14 How Anxiety Travels Through Generations 107

CHAPTER 15 Birth Order, Personality, and Relationships 111

CHAPTER 16 Societal Chaos and the Family 115

PART THREE

PARENTS CONNECTING

CHAPTER 17 Present and Accounted For 127

CHAPTER 18 The Emotional Nucleus—
the Parents' Relationship. 133

CHAPTER 19 Connecting with Our Children 139

CHAPTER 20 Ages and Stages of Family Life 149

CHAPTER 21 The Single Parent and Combined Families. 165

CHAPTER 22 Play, Self-Regulation, and the Many
Ways to Deal with Anxiety 175

CHAPTER 23 Family Life as a Spiritual Journey 185

CHAPTER 24 On Being a Self in the Generations. 189

CHAPTER 25 In Conclusion—a Personal Note 199

Notes 203

APPENDIX 1 Reading Resources 209

APPENDIX 2 Psychotherapy Resources 211

Index. 221

Acknowledgments

I want to at least try to express all the gratitude that is in me to the following people:

Murray Bowen, in spirit and memory, for giving us all this wonderful theory that is truly a new way of seeing relationships and the human world;

Leroy Bowen for her thoughtful reading of this manuscript and useful comments, and for sharing precious history;

Joanne Bowen for reading the manuscript and making extensive and thoughtful comments that were most helpful;

Carolyn Zolbe, the "Guardian of the English Language," and good friend, for her careful reading and extremely useful comments;

Frank Giove for his careful and useful reading;

Patricia Hyland for reading;

Dave Gilbert for reading and encouraging, as he does so often in life;

Greg Jacobs for reading, approving enthusiastically, and for teaching, always;

Carroll Hoskins for reading and making helpful comments;

Claudia Barlow for working with me in many ways, but especially for placing this manuscript in the right hands, and for her thoughtful reading;

Claire Lewis, Cheryl Kimball, David Enyeart, and all others, whether I know them or not, involved with the publishing of this book at Chronimed Publishing, the only publishers I know of who understand there is a readership for something different than "quick fix" and "big name";

Joseph Douglass, Jr., my husband, for teaching me so much about how better to write a book, how to focus for a long time or short term, and a great deal about being there as a partner in life.

A Personal Foreword

Most people, having become parents, want very much to do an excellent job at that all-important role. We want to give our children a better life than we have ourselves. To that end, we provide every material, educational, and cultural advantage money can buy. We eagerly schedule soccer, ballet, art, music lessons, and car pools. We try to move to neighborhoods that have good school systems and good people. We fill our homes with books, toys, TVs, and computers. Yet, it seems that many of us are missing the mark. Somehow we feel we are not doing very well at being parents. And, in fact, perhaps some of us are not. What is getting in the way?

Even though we probably have, under ordinary circumstances, what it takes to become excellent parents, most of us were not prepared for the overwhelming effects on our families of the gradual and increasing breakdown of society itself. This snowballing phenomenon, intruding more and more into our everyday lives, is making the job of being a parent increasingly more difficult than it was for our parents or their parents. Dangerously addictive street drugs are increasingly common and easily available to young schoolchildren. Crime and violence make going to school dangerous. The schools themselves seem to be adding to the problems families face with an emphasis on feelings over thinking, and, often seeing parents as the problem, turning their children against them unnecessarily.

Parents, working to provide for what are considered necessities and to meet personal goals, often find themselves abandoning their children to their own devices for several hours out of the working day. This presents an unprecedented challenge for today's families, whether headed up by one or two parents.

A thinking person will look for a way out of the morass. Efforts often take the form of activities, interest groups, and day care for the children, and therapy or support groups for the parents. Considering all that is available to parents, I have come to believe that what is usually left out of the planning may be the most significant thing of all: relationships. Relationships with each other as parents, and with our children shed light on much of the problem when we focus on the family as the basic emotional unit.

Perhaps a natural enough reaction is for us not to think much about relationships, because many, if not most, American families are probably the culmination of many generations of "cutoff"—that automatic retreat into relationship distance. Often, we did not have satisfying relationships with our parents, nor did they with theirs, and so it seems to be "just the way it is done." We automatically carry that cutoff posture into the relationship with our own children. Many people know no other way of being in a family.

Even if we are not cut off from the younger generation, seldom are we proficient at the "relationship part" of being a parent. We tend to focus on our kids too much or not enough. We fight with them, boss them around, or depend on them too much. Often we ask for third-party advice when what we really need is to clearly understand what it is we ourselves actually think about a given issue.

After several years in psychiatric practice, I was growing increasingly dissatisfied. One of the sources of my dissatisfaction was the fact that parents were bringing me their children and teenagers, asking me to "fix" them. Their children were drinking, taking drugs, and getting bad grades, or were simply out of control in a variety of ways. My training had been excellent, but try as I would, I had the feeling that the therapy I conducted was not really having much of an impact on these young people. Slowly it began to dawn on me that these youngsters did not need to be fixed. What was broken and needing help was the entire family unit.

To pursue this idea and to learn more about the human family, I became an eager student in a post-graduate training program in family therapy. That training was useful, and the families I worked with began to benefit from it. Family therapy was a great improvement over the methods I had been taught earlier, which emphasized the individual with little concern about how people interacted with one other. However, my results were still not what I wanted them to be. I still did not have a way to think about the family as a whole; that is, as an organism. It was at this point that I discovered Dr. Murray Bowen, and graduated from family therapy to family theory.

As early as the 1940s, Dr. Bowen had begun thinking about the family—rather than the individual—as the true "emotional unit." This radical departure from conventional theory saw the problem in the family and its interactional patterns rather than solely in the individual at a time when the analyst/therapist, on principle, usually had no contact at all with family members.

I had little understanding of what Bowen was proposing when I first started to listen. However, my frustration was increasing as I tried, myself, to be an effective parent as well as help other families, so I decided to listen more closely. Suddenly, I found his ideas incredibly useful, not only in the lives of my patients but in my own as well. The new theoretical framework, so clearly revealing the family rather than the individual as the basic organism, was exactly what I had been searching for.

"Emotional cutoff" was one of the first Bowen family systems theory ideas I was able to really hear. Cutoff is the most extreme form of emotional distance, where people have little or no meaningful emotional contact. I watched as people with long-term symptoms of family disconnect, such as depression, began to work on their cutoffs. They had dramatic results. Some went off antidepressant medications they had been on for years. Others were able to discontinue more expensive and unsatisfactory forms of psychotherapy. I watched kids' symptoms disappear as parents began to relate more effectively to each other and to the children.

Having worked in Bowen family systems theory for a number of years, I have come to the conclusion that *the need to understand relationships is the single biggest issue in our society.* Personal relationships are the key to individual success and to launching the next generation. Basic aptitudes for forming meaningful and workable relationships are taken on by our children as they grow up in our families. More than ever before, we must understand something about our families and their relationships to address individual problems, and especially to rear children in today's environment.

Further, I believe that society will continue to disintegrate if people do not have a principled way of relating between and among the generations. Many of society's huge problems concerning the homeless, gangs and cults, violence, addictions, divorce, teenage pregnancy, and even chronic physical illness trace their origins to the relationship system—the family—and its interactions. My effort to make a difference in all of this is to let people know about principles that have been useful to parents as they have tried to be their best with their babies, young children, teenagers, and young adults—as well as with each other and their own parents.

Part of what I have learned is that being an effective parent in a time of turmoil is intimately connected to the relationships we have and have had with each of our own parents, the rest of our family of origin, and the generations that preceded them. We can only be as good parents as we are sons and daughters. That does not mean perfection. It only means that we take seriously the challenge of relating to our own parents and extended families. Through this effort, our skills as parents increase dramatically.

Examples in this book are composites taken from the many families I have connected with over the years, including my own. Names and distinguishing characteristics have been changed where necessary to protect individuals' identities.

While this book draws heavily on Bowen family systems theory, presented at an introductory level, it is theory as understood and used by this one practitioner, not necessarily as Bowen or any other theorist has understood or applied Bowen theory. Each person's understanding and application of theory must be uniquely his or her own. Therefore, there will always be shades of difference as different people understand and use Bowen theory.

In this work I include areas not formally included in Bowen theory—for example, humor and spirituality—because I personally believe them to be of great importance. I do not remember Dr. Bowen saying much about humor although he was great at bringing it into play. He did attempt to make spirituality a part of formal theory at one time but when his efforts were not well received by the profession, he did not pursue the subject any further. However, he was intrigued with the prayer of St. Francis and he found Bowen family systems theory in it!

Bowen's driving mission was to design a theoretical construct that would bring the study of human behavior into the realm of the accepted sciences. He saw the *family as an emotional unit*—the reality that had been overlooked by traditional theory as it focused on the individual. To test out that pivotal realization he hospitalized whole families at the National Institutes of Health. Not only was Bowen family systems theory first tested there but also many other developments and refinements were worked out there as well. He spent the rest of his life on family theory, writing, speaking, and teaching about it. He pioneered the use of videotapes in clinical and didactic teaching. But it is probably accurate to say that family theory is still in its infancy. The task of further development, research, extension, and refinement of the theory was left to others.

Because of my years of association with the Georgetown Family Center where Dr. Bowen did so much of his teaching, writing, and clinical work, I have come to know many of those "others" who trained there and then took seriously the task of continuing to work on the theory. Their ideas and work are exciting and interesting. I could not leave them out of this book. I called on those I knew of who had presented and written on subjects important to parents. They responded to my request for participation quickly and enthusiastically. Their thinking is scattered throughout these pages. Their thoughts should be taken as theirs, and mine as mine, and not part of any particularly pure or more special version of theory nor one that Bowen himself would have especially endorsed. Receiving the contributions from all these people was energizing and uplifting.

If I omitted anyone who should have been included, it was not intentional. Some declined, and some I simply didn't know about. This book is not the only or final word. There is much more available! I have included resources for further exploration.

The reader may wish to refer to my earlier book on Bowen theory, *Extraordinary Relationships*. Its glossary and appendices may be of especial interest. To continue study, one can refer to other texts and a journal, which are listed in an appendix.

It is impossible to gain anything but the barest introduction to Bowen family systems theory from a book alone. People who take these ideas seriously and want to apply them for themselves in their own family and work groups find they need a psychotherapist from time to time. Therapy implies to many that the therapist does something to the family that helps it. Some use "coach" or "consultant" because the burden is on the individual in the family to do the work or take the ball and run with it.

Because traditional theories are much more prevalent, it is often not easy to find a person trained in Bowen family systems theory when one is needed. For that reason I have included in an appendix a directory of people who have made a serious effort on Bowen family systems theory—learning it, applying it, and contributing to it over time. If they themselves are inaccessible it is my hope that they can serve to direct people further.

Time, and experience in life, will tell whether any particular effort is true to the way things really are. If a description is accurate over time then it is properly a part of a theory that attempts to describe the human phenomenon as accurately and broadly as possible.

Some of the questions I had in mind as I wrote were:

What have Bowen family systems students, clinicians, and theorists learned that might help parents cope with the difficult situations families face today?

What guidelines does theory provide as we think about relating to the next generation?

What do I wish I had known as my children were growing up?

With those questions in mind I constructed the book in three parts. In Part One, we look at the problems in society—many unique and intense—and the problems they create for parents today, as well as the age-old difficulties within families themselves.

Part Two is designed as a short presentation of Bowen family systems theory for parents. It is only by looking at all the problems in a new and more comprehensive way—through a different lens—that we will find a way out. Surely the traditional approaches have not been useful.

Part Three describes what I see as I watch myself and many other parents in their ongoing efforts to try to put these principles into practice in life. I am eager to tell what I have learned and am still learning about relating better to the next generation, using a "new way of thinking about human interaction."

Part One

Rearing Children
in a
Troubled World

What in the World
Is Happening?

Parents are the hope of civilization.

Much depends on whether parents can connect in a meaningful, positive way with each other and with their children. If they can, a generation may emerge ready to tackle and reverse some ominous trends.

Connecting With Our Children presents a way of thinking that parents can use to help them form the crucial connections. These connections can make the difference between things as they are, things getting worse, and hope for the future. The ideas set forth have already become guiding principles for many families in the United States.

But first, what is happening in our world?

The world is different for today's parents. It is different from the world of their parents and perhaps from the world of any parents ever before. When we ourselves grew up we could play in our back yards unsupervised for long stretches. We walked to school or the school bus in safety. The most dangerous substance anyone ever offered us was, perhaps, a sip of beer. We spent a significant part of each day with one or both parents. They had time for us. We took family vacations and ate family meals together. It never occurred to us to go out on school nights. Pregnancy in high school was unusual.

None of these things holds true in the world we live in now. In one generation it has become dangerous for anyone to be on many of our city streets alone. Young children must always be supervised. Metal detectors and other security measures are commonplace in schools. Children are in contact with dangerous and illegal drugs at younger and younger ages. Sexual impulses are indulged rather than respected, so that children feel obliged to alter their hormonal systems with birth control medications. Abstinence is rarely suggested. Movies, TV, magazines, and the internet make childhood and teen sex seem ordinary. Parents, doctors, and educators deliver the final approval with prescriptions and birth control gifts.

In a PBS production on violence, Bill Moyers pointed out that because of television, video games, and computers, we are rearing our children with increasingly less human contact. In this way we promote isolation, which undermines human family relationships.

The *Index of Leading Cultural Indicators* reports that over the last three decades we have experienced "substantial social regression," which is defined as: "there has been a 560 percent increase in violent crime; more than a 400 percent increase in illegitimate births; a quadrupling in divorce rates; a tripling of the percentage of children living in single-parent homes; more than a 200 percent increase in the teenage suicide rate; and a drop of almost 80 points in the S.A.T. scores (though the population has increased only 41 percent)."

A 1990 report by a special commission of prominent political, medical, education, and business leaders, titled *Code Blue,* examined the health of America's teenagers. They wrote that "never before has one generation of American teenagers been less healthy, less cared for, or less prepared for life than their parents were at the same age."

Another disturbing sign of declining conditions among the young is a teacher survey. Over the years teachers were asked to identify the top problems in America's public schools. In 1940, teachers identified talking out of turn; chewing gum; making noise; running in the halls; cutting in line; dress code infractions; and littering. Asked the same question in 1990, teachers identified drug abuse; alcohol abuse; pregnancy; suicide; rape; robbery; and assault.

Drugs—illegal, dangerous, addictive drugs—are now one of the world's largest industries.

The "Add Health Study," from the National Institutes of Health and two medical schools, found that one quarter of teens are current smokers, one in six drink alcohol more than once a month, and nearly one third smoke marijuana. Columbia University reports "After dropping steadily from 1979 to 1992, adolescent marijuana use jumped more than 80 percent over the next two years."

Moreover, most statistics on drug use understate the severity of the problem because they are based on self reports. Though assumed accurate, they are not. For example, at a walk-in medical clinic of Emery University, of 160 men who tested positive for cocaine, only 28.1 percent had admitted to illicit drug use within the prior 72 hours and only 45.6 percent had admitted to illicit drug use within the prior week. Because respondents lie, surveys that depend on self reporting to garner statistics, therefore, usually provide severe underestimations of actual use.

Joseph Califano, Secretary of Health, Education, and Welfare in the Carter Administration and top aide for domestic affairs for President Lyndon B. Johnson, reported that "federal entitlement programs linked to drug, alcohol and tobacco abuse were about $70 billion in 1997." He believes that, "The road to a drug free America lies not in the executive agencies, congressional committees and government programs, but in our children and their parents. There is a lot of work that needs to be done on that road. *And most of that work is a mom and pop operation.*"

Crime apparently pays in today's world. Since 1960 criminal activity has increased over 300 percent. Leading Cultural Indicators says that the fastest growing segment of the criminal population is our nation's children. The Federal Bureau of Investigation reports that the nearly quadrupling in juvenile arrests has involved not only the "disadvantaged minority youth in urban areas but all races, all social classes and life styles."

Fully 16 percent of 7th and 8th graders and almost half of the 9th to 12th graders report that they have experienced sexual intercourse, according to the N.I.H.'s largest study ever made of adolescents. The number of pregnancies among unmarried teenagers has nearly doubled in the last two decades. The American Enterprise Institute reports that teenage sexual activity will result in nearly one million pregnancies annually, 406,000 abortions, 134,000 miscarriages, and 490,000 live births.

Children are becoming pregnant at a rate that makes it impossible for social welfare institutions to deal with them. A head of such an agency reported they could not meet the need. They could find no acceptable answer for the problem of children having babies, too young to exist on their own, refusing to allow adoption, and being refused support by their own parents.

Yet another indicator of where society is—the teen suicide rate—is highlighted in *Leading Cultural Indicators.* "The rate at which teenagers are taking their own lives is increasing rapidly. Since 1960, the teen suicide rate has more than tripled. *Suicide is now the third leading cause of death among adolescents*—behind motor vehicle accidents and all other accidents." Edward Zigler from Yale University notes that for every successful adolescent suicide there are fifty to one hundred attempts. This means that more than 5 percent of all teenagers tried to take their lives in 1990, compared with 1 percent in 1960.

Dissolution of families is the rule rather than the exception in our society. This means single-parent and blended families (parts of two former nuclear families combining to make a new nuclear unit) are redefining what "family" means. Two-career families, an economic necessity in large cities, complicate life for parents. In 1991, less than 60 percent of children were living with their biological, married parents. In large cities in 1991, around 50 percent of children were living in single-parent homes.

Society's institutions are confused about their roles. Schools, for example, have taken on a new task, that of the psychological and life adjustment of the students. As a part of that effort, teachers will often ask children to write journal entries about their feelings and problems. But the teachers then say they do not know what to do with what the children write. Further, feelings are a questionable area for continued focus, especially by the untrained, so the schools in such well-meaning efforts may be actually adding to the problem. In these projects, aimed at helping children emotionally, both children and teachers are sometimes left confused and anxious, unable to focus on traditional school tasks the rest of the day. In addition, these efforts often have the outcome of polarizing kids against their parents.

Courts, not wanting to make the problem worse for children in dissolving, conflicted families, don't know how or where to place responsibility. One judge's poignant statement, in his findings regarding the disputed custody of a child, puts it very well: "For lawyers and judges alike there are not a lot of things, other than common sense and experience, to help guide them and give them a list of do's and dont's about how to handle parent/child relationships. Lawyers and judges only have the tools that they are given by the experience of dealing with these cases, their own experiences as parents, and formerly as children in the earlier part of their lives, to help them wade through probably the most complex relationship between human beings, that being the relationship between parents and their children."

Emotional Process in Society

One of the formal concepts of Bowen family systems theory, *emotional process in society*, is sometimes also called *societal regression*. It means that society is more or less anxious, orderly, and organized at different times in history. In times of societal regression, there is more anxiety in all people, firing chaos and irresponsibility in society. In turn, the chaos and irresponsibility create more anxiety, leading to more problems in society, in an escalating cycle.

In a more anxious or regressive time individuals are under a great deal more stress. Institutions of society, including families, are less organized and stable. They are more subject to breakdowns, dissolutions, and reorganizations. Thus, in families we see separations and divorce statistics growing. With both parents out of the home most of the time, no one has quite figured out how to best bring up children. "Latchkey kids," unsupervised before they are ready, exhibit various problems. The frequent reconfigurations and reductions in force in organizations can be seen as another outworking of societal anxiety. Often there is little or no notice given to the terminated workers. These and other evidences such as repeated takeovers and mergers, overtly or covertly planned, friendly or hostile, cause tremendous stress for those involved.

All of these regressive and chaotic forces produce intense stresses on individuals and families. A breadwinner going to work only to find out that he or she has no position, effective immediately, develops tremendous anxiety about loss of status, self respect, and income as well as the pressure of looking for another job. These anxieties quickly spread through the whole family, leading to strains on relationships. If the family dissolves under the pressure, the family problem increases enormously.

Parents seem to have no principled way to think about leading themselves and their families through our turbulent times. About the best most of them can do is to invoke principles that guided their parents. If they are lucky enough to have come from a high-functioning family, their parents' principles may work well for them too. However, in many cases, simply relying on principles of a former time may or may not lead to positive outcomes.

What are some of the factors that may have helped bring about a society in regression? Many possible root causes of the anxiety leading to it have been cited. For example, one may be the population explosion with its attendant scarcity of land and other resources. Others may also be at work—anxiety over the threat of annihilation by nuclear, chemical, or biological weapons, epidemics such as AIDS, diversity of peoples trying to live together, and economic forces that may be increasing anxiety in large numbers of people. The teachings of the predominant forces in the world of therapy itself may have played a part in bringing on the regressive society. Ideas popularized in this manner such as "permissiveness" and "the pleasure principle" may, in some families, have reinforced tendencies toward irresponsibility. No doubt many of these factors play some part.

The Problem Within

Not only is society presenting parents with unique, new, and intensely difficult problems, but there are also problems within ourselves and our families that are as old as life on earth. The immaturity in each of us can also be seen as a big part of the reason our society—and our families—are in trouble. The more emotionally stable parents among us would be thinking and acting more from their own principles than those of their family or even the society around them. They would have a bigger, more accurate view of the size and shape of the human problem as well as their own. They would not be as vulnerable to the teachings of permissiveness and instant gratification, or their opposites, over-authoritarian stances. Most of us, though, are not able to think through teachings of respected authorities for ourselves, deciding whether or not they are logical or applicable to us. In the same way we would often simply be adopting our parents' teachings and styles—or reacting against them, rather than doing the hard work of thinking things through for ourselves.

So, the roots of society's problem can also be traced to parents themselves, who, having no better guiding principles, adopted some that were taught by a respected profession or a former generation. In accepting permissiveness and pleasure as basic values, and in not thinking all the way through to their own values, it seems that many parents acquiesced to a profession or their parents, instead of opting for a more responsible position in one of life's most important roles.

Under conditions of regression in society and in a majority of individuals the immaturity in people wins out. Bowen theory psychotherapist, Andrea Maloney-Schara thinks that the small nuclear family's distance from its family of origin has induced families' demanding and irresponsible behavior, where the most demanding one wins. As pressure is put on wives to work, wives put pressure on husbands to help out. Children then put pressure on parents to pay attention. With larger numbers of single-parent families, as they move away from their home communities, there are fewer extended family members to help out. Automatically, stress plays itself out in drugs, affairs, conflict, distance, or physical symptoms in one or many family members. She notes that the ability to maintain family relationships may be more challenging than that of providing for basic survival needs.

It is clear, in thinking about how beliefs guide our behavior, both as professionals and as parents, that how we think makes a great difference in how we act and what we do. For example, if we think that permissiveness is necessary to rearing healthy kids, then we will let the kids get by with behavior that we would not otherwise. If the pleasure principle is espoused as a value of life, and interpreted to mean short-term immediate pleasure, then pleasure for its own sake will be sought and, paradoxically, sacrifices may be endured in order to attain it—pay for the Disney vacation or the designer clothes. When people are guided by the pleasure principle, drugs, alcohol, and promiscuity that give short-term pleasure may not be recognized for the long-term threat they pose.

At this time, when so many young people and society itself seem to be running amok, it is absolutely necessary to rethink our guiding principles. The current ones from the therapy professions, and others we've been taught, may not be serving us well. Rather, much of this traditional theory seems to have helped to bring about the problems we now face. Thoughtful parents, if there is any hope for society, need to begin to do that most difficult work of all-thinking. They need to think about what it is they really believe, until they get all the way through to clarity and to a higher ground.

One psychotherapist, Frank Giove, finds that most parents anxiously want him to fix the problem. They have trouble looking at themselves in thoughtful ways. Since there are no quick fixes for most situations, he tries to reveal the reciprocal postures in the family. If one or both parents will see his or her own part in the back and forth flow of the family relationships, they can make some progress toward change.

In a society that is not working, with principles that don't work, and contending with their own inner immaturity, many parents are at a loss as to how to think about one of the most important tasks in life— that of being a parent.

For many successful parents, the ideas of Bowen family systems theory formulate a better foundation for relationships—the all-important factor in rearing the young—than we have had until now. Parents using these ideas as a framework find they can give their children the best possible legacy—that of a principled way of being in relationships.

Now, let's take a look at how problems develop in the next generation.

How Problems Develop in Young People

When the nuclear family is seen as an emotional unit, a child is only a part of that unit—a fragment of the larger whole. Part of what that means is that an action, attitude, or emotion of one person in the group affects everyone else in it. Because any family member is only a part of a larger entity, children with problems are rarely the underlying problem. Rather, they are symptoms of something much bigger—a family emotional or relationship problem. In order to understand that larger difficulty, let us consider how anxiety travels in a group of people.

Anxiety visibly passes between and among people in a family group. It is not hard to see this going on. If Dad comes home upset because an important proposal he made at work was rejected, he may begin to "take it out" on Mom, criticizing and accusing her of not living up to his standards of child or house care (see figure 1).

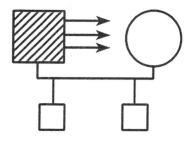

FIGURE 1

Mom may try to justify what she thinks and does angrily or tear-fully, or she may shut down, sad, quiet. In either case, Dad's anxiety has now moved to Mom (see figure 2).

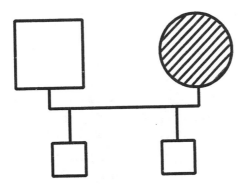

FIGURE 2

Next, the three-year-old, seeing his mother's distress, may begin to cry. The anxiety has moved to him (see figure 3).

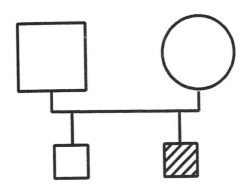

FIGURE 3

Their six-year-old, noticing the emotional intensity, goes immediately to his room. The anxiety has now moved to him (see figure 4).

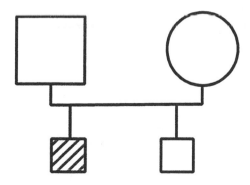

FIGURE 4

In this way, anxiety moves from person to person in a family unit. Sometimes there is enough anxiety to upset everyone in the group (see figure 5).

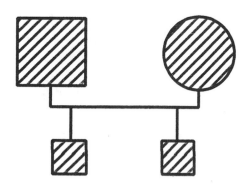

FIGURE 5

Often, however, rather than disturbing the entire group, anxiety seems to settle in one person. Often that person is a child. For example, although the original anxiety exchange was between the two parents, if they don't get it worked out over time and and if the tearful three-year-old continues to cry long, hard, and often enough, he or she will begin to draw the focus of the adults. Not realizing his anxious crying really is an expression of anxiety displaced from them and their unsolved relationship difficulties, they may come to see their child as having a problem. They will begin to worry about him, and may take him for professional help.

In this way, if the adults in a family have a problem they do not deal with and resolve, anxiety gets displaced to a child. As the child becomes an anxiety sink for the family, he or she will definitely develop some kind of problem. When that happens and the adults in the family begin to focus on the child and his or her problem, two things ensue. First, they never get around to resolving their own relationship dilemma(s). In addition, the child who is being focused upon develops a problem (see figure 6).

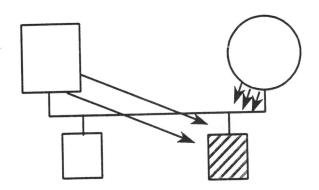

FIGURE 6

If this process continues over time and becomes a pattern, the child's problem draws more anxious focus from his or her parents. The anxious focus intensifies the anxiety residing in the child, which intensifies the problem, and so on and on.

When anxiety mounts in an individual, brain and body chemistry become altered. Behavior and even anatomy may change. The child may show overactivity; underactivity; behavior, learning, or physical health problems; or act socially inappropriately. Or, the brain chemistry changes associated with anxiety may produce mental and emotional symptoms and/or other formal disorders or syndromes. By not dealing with their own conflicts, the parents have moved anxiety that properly belongs with them to a child. They feel better. The child feels worse. Performance and/ or emotional or emotional health may decline.

Once an identifiable illness or disorder develops, more and more intense—sometimes lifelong—focus is drawn to the problem from the family and the professionals. The problem intensifies the anxiety and the anxiety of the family about the problem intensifies the problem in a vicious cycle that is hard to interrupt.

Society for its part may provide increasing opportunity for symptom development. As anxiety mounts in society, it, of course, mounts in individuals and family groups. The media seem to do their part to promote anxiety. Since anxiety from different sources is cumulative, this will add to the usual family burden of anxiety.

Society in regression also provides more and more dangerous opportunities for vulnerable young people. As the regressive conditions intensify, they feed on themselves. Drugs, alcohol, sex, guns, and cars, made more and more available by regressed and permissive families and society, mean that young people have to travel increasingly more dangerous roads in life.

A world in regression also provides a kind of pressure for families toward perceiving regressive decisions and behavior as "the norm." Many families, for example, feel completely helpless in the face of strong pressures from young people to be out late at night with their friends, especially in the summer, and sometimes even during the school year.

Parents with a guidance system made up of their own principles, however, have an advantage in making decisions, in forming relationships, and in guiding their own lives and the direction of their families. Their principles will show the way to a calmer, more thoughtful stance than that provided by the regressive society. At times they must take a stand and go against the tide of society as well as pressures of their kids and their peers. Without principles, the parent is hard pressed to answer "why" in a meaningful manner when asked. When parents become overly anxious about their child, with principles they can "step back," consider the situation, and decide to take more of the focus back to management of themselves and their own adult relationships. Their clearheadedness and the gift of principles in life make for better decisions and smoother relationships, so the family does better in many areas. For example, the newspapers provide multiple opportunities to discuss societal problems as well as beliefs and principles with one's children. It is even possible for the regressive conditions in society to act as a stimulus for some families to do better. Now let us consider a few examples of the more common symptoms that develop in children as family anxiety focuses on, and comes to rest in, any particular child.

Why Johnny Isn't Learning

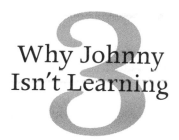

When Johnny was born, his father was not at all sure he wanted another child. He was satisfied enough with the one child he and his wife already had. And he was going through a lot of problems at work. He was not at all sure his job would last. Johnny's mother had prevailed, however, and their second child was born. Johnny was an easy child as a toddler, and lots of fun. However, by the time he was in school, his parents' relationship had turned to one of conflict and distance, by turns. Johnny and his father alternated being angry at, or ignoring each other—not the kind of relationship either wanted. His mother saw to Johnny's physical needs but remained at a kind of emotional distance from her children much of the time, because she was so distracted by her own marital distress. Her distant posture was part of the problem between herself and her own family of origin. This distance intensified anxiety in the family she had helped to create. She had no way to understand her young family's lack of relationship success as somehow related to the relationship problems in her original family.

As his parents' relationship problem intensified, Johnny went to school with higher and higher levels of anxiety. Johnny's "easy" disposition became tearful and whiny at times and at other times provocative, as he poked the other children or distracted them in other ways. The high level of anxiety reverberating in his brain meant that he literally did not hear much of what the teacher said. He was "not there" for much of class, which interfered with his ability to learn to read and write.

Diagnostic tests were not much help, only revealing a "developmental lag." That is, his brain had no basic brain dysfunction nor disability that testing could reveal. His parents were assured that he would eventually catch up. But the tester had no way to ferret out the larger family relationship problem at the root of his distractibility and underachievement. So his parents, instead of focusing on their own difficulties in relating to each other, began to focus on Johnny and his "problem" more. They never did resolve their own conflicts. Had they done this, it might have made a tremendous difference not only in their own lives, but in Johnny's as well.

As his "learning problem" continued on through the grades of elementary school, Johnny lost whatever self-esteem he started out with. He associated with children far below his family's social level and his own intelligence level. These friends helped set the stage for more problems to come.

There are many reasons why children can't or don't achieve in school. Most of them, this author is convinced, have to do with family anxiety. Sophisticated testing may reveal brain dysfunction but is not geared to measure or identify how the family emotional relationship system adds to an existing problem by its worried focus or, in some cases, can initiate it. If a child goes to school with a certain level of anxiety he or she has absorbed from the family, it is difficult, if not impossible, for him or her to concentrate on the classroom content. The cerebral cortex does not function logically and thoughtfully in the presence of a great deal of anxiety, so these children don't meet deadlines, forget to hand in their assignments, or have a difficult time organizing books, papers, and time.

Sometimes the kids actually are learning, as achievement tests on Johnny eventually showed. However, they don't get through all the hoops required by school very well. If homework is always late or missing, or tests not prepared for, grades are affected.

Also, relationships, disordered at home, are also disorderly at school. The family relationships, if intense and disturbed, create a pattern the child replicates with his or her peers. In addition, the anxiety the child takes to school each day adversely affects the relation-

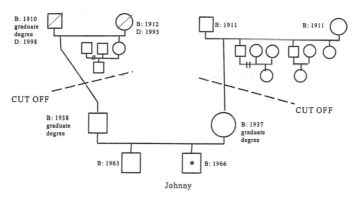

JOHNNY'S FAMILY DIAGRAM

ships he or she is trying to form there. If children experience conflict and distance between the adults at home they will usually carry those relationship patterns and that anxiety with them when they try to form relationships outside the home.

A PBS documentary questioned the diagnosis of ADD and ADHD for children who used to be called lazy, bored, or distracted, noting that the use of the label is spreading, along with the use of powerful psychostimulants, for example, Ritalin. It stated that there are now an estimated two million children on these agents, with the number doubling every two years.

David Drake, a family systems-oriented psychiatrist, in discussing this problem, points out that the list of behaviors associated with attention deficit and hyperactivity are identical to those associated with anxiety. Dr. Drake believes that anxious families or clinicians are likely to focus on one individual alone as having the problem. He emphasizes to parents that the child's behavior is symptomatic of a "stirred-up family" and will prescribe medication for these children only if one parent is willing to consider his or her own contribution to the family problem. As the formerly calm marriage becomes the object of inquiry, tensions rise between the parents. At that point the child will often calm down.

However, if the parents take their focus off the marriage, themselves, and their families of origin, then the focus predictably returns to the child again as the problem. At that point, Dr. Drake finds the child exhibits symptoms once again!

Societal Regression and the Schools

Because many schools themselves are involved in the whirlpool of societal regression, schools offer no escape for children. As Dan Papero, an educator and therapist, and Robert Felton, an educator, have pointed out in a presentation, school administrators now have to deal with individual parents or parent groups with strong views on various issues, often to the point of having to be involved in several lawsuits at once. They have little time to actually run the school because of all the side issues constantly taking time and attention.

The Columbia University Center on Addiction and Substance Abuse describes the situation well:

> A national survey of high school honor students revealed that drinking beer, smoking, drinking hard liquor and using marijuana followed only alternative music as the top five 'in' things at their schools. Drugs and alcohol have changed the way students in urban America go to and from school and learn in the classroom. In many junior high and high schools, children pass through security more stringent than at airports. To enter, they must remove their belts, pass through metal detectors and have their backpacks x-rayed by security guards. Each day, guards and teachers confiscate switchblades, razors, guns and box cutters. School principals lock bathrooms to prevent smoking and drug use and dealing.

> "For many American school children, safely getting to school in the morning and getting home in the afternoon is a frightening challenge. Drug dealers troll the streets for young customers. Alcoholics and addicts, including many homeless, intimidate children. Shootouts between rival gangs, often over drug turf, catch innocent children in deadly crossfire. Students have been so regularly harassed, robbed and frightened that police departments from Austin, Texas, to New York, New York, have been forced to carve out 'safe corridors,' which are street routes the police encourage students to use when traveling to and from school. The police promise to patrol these streets more closely; they cannot guarantee the safety of other routes to school."

Weapons are being taken to school and outbreaks of violence on the premises and illegal drugs put school officials in an almost impossible position in many places. They are unable to provide basic functions or guarantee safety. These kinds of issues can generate a "red alert" level of anxiety in the entire school system (as they do in a family). So in these ways schools, one of society's most basic organizations, are, themselves, manifesting the regression that is currently in full swing.

Clearly, society's regressive cycle affects the family by adding to its load of anxiety. A child's anxiety, given the current situation at school and in the neighborhood, may originate there and not in the family at all. Parents must be aware of all this. But families are especially vulnerable to damage by the breakdowns in society if they have no guiding principles of their own that can help point the way through the morass. They can lose their footing and even their identity as a family if, as one family member put it, the "nuclear family goes through a nuclear meltdown" and divorces. If, on the other hand, the adults in the family can begin to work on:

- the facts of a situation,
- their relationships with each other, and
- getting clear about their own beliefs,

they will find ways to assist a symptomatic child out of the fog and guide their own family group to more solid ground.

Parents can often assist and encourage in the learning process. A parent, merely by being calmly interested in daily homework, and actually looking it over every day, can take a step up in functioning—being there for the child in a way that shows non-anxious interest. Kids who complete their homework and hand it in on time usually do well on tests. It can be that simple.

A parent can begin to show and express confidence in the child rather than worry about him. Worrying about the child, as we have seen, only adds to the load of anxiety that generated the child's problem in the first place. Worry or anxiety is not something parents can hide. Children can easily tell when parents are anxious and worried about them. Replacing worry with confidence can be a first step in relating differently.

These parents can get clearer on what can and cannot be reasonably expected of their child, when he or she needs encouragement, and when the child needs space. Even more important, they can get their own relationship on track, so that the entire family has to cope with less displaced anxiety.

Irresponsible Behavior and Substance Abuse

The more Johnny's family's anxiety intensified and his parents headed toward divorce, the worse he felt inside. As the years went by, his own relationship dilemmas intensified. He often seemed to be hanging out with the "wrong" people. His parents, always trying to help him, tried school after school, since he had so many complaints about each one. They hoped the right school with the right teachers and away from the influence of "the wrong kind of friends" could get their son headed down the right track. But in school after school the problems and patterns were the same.

They were unable to recognize how their unresolved family relationship dilemmas were fundamental to Johnny's difficulties—nor did anyone they consulted for counseling know how to look at this bigger picture. They were aware that their own relationship was not functioning well, but they eventually came to hope that a divorce would help that. Perhaps it would give them both a new start and everyone in the family a breath of fresh air, they reasoned. They were sure that they did not want their problems to affect the kids, whom they loved. But Johnny's relationship with his dad was conflictual and that with his mom distant. These two postures reflected the two postures his parents took, alternately, with each other.

After the divorce things went from bad to worse. Angry, foul language from Johnny became commonplace and he occasionally acted out in anger, even damaging furniture. Johnny was kicked out of several schools for bad behavior. During high school he sometimes left school to hang out with friends and smoke marijuana. Though he graduated from high school, college was impossible because by then he had gone on to more regular drug use, making any serious academic effort impossible.

The point is often made that children with acting-out problems really have at base a learning disability and that the behavior problems are only an outgrowth of a lack of achievement in school. Seen through the lens of Bowen family systems theory, it is more likely that both learning and behavior difficulties are symptomatic of, or exacerbated by troubled family relationships. When the family system starts to work better—with more cooperation and less anxiety—the children often lose both their behavior and learning symptoms over time.

The effects of marijuana are commonly represented as benign. This is far from the case, as outlined by the Columbia Center: "It impairs short-term memory and judgment, induces anxiety, distorts perception and diminishes motor skills." The junior high and high school years represent a peak time of intellectual, physical, and emotional development, a crucial time when the brain can be particularly vulnerable to toxic agents. Yet many young people at this age seem to have accepted the myth that marijuana is safe. Extremely few understand its true dangers.

The Center's research indicates that a 12- to 17-year-old who smokes cigarettes is 19 times more likely to use cocaine than an individual who does not; one who drinks, 50 times; and one who smokes pot, 85 times.

It also finds that drug and alcohol abuse are joined at the hip with the violence that threatens today's children, both as perpetrators and as victims. Juvenile and family court judges find substance abuse a significant factor in 60 to 90 percent of cases. More than 80 percent of juvenile offenders have used illegal drugs, and AIDS and other sexually transmitted diseases are often transmitted during the irresponsible sexual behavior associated with adolescent drug and alcohol use.

Anne McKnight, working with families who have a substance-abusing teenager, believes alcohol and drugs are used by some teens to separate from their parents. In the world of substance abuse (including their using friends), they find an identity that is independent of that of their family. The problem with this rebellious way of separating is that in the end many of the young people develop symptoms from the drugs or alcohol and become more dependent on their parents than before. In this way the substance use becomes a problem that takes on a life of its own.

McKnight emphasizes that once the person develops symptoms owing to the direct and/or damaging effects of the substances, they may need direct and specific attention for recovery to begin. Some useful interventions include, in addition to family relationship coaching, detoxification treatment and educational information regarding the process and problem. Sometimes residential care may be needed. All of these can be useful at the right time for selected people.

One of the most difficult problems our society faces is that of children having children. Irene Morin had oversight responsibility for an agency that tried to lend a hand to these children. Here are a few of the facts she discovered: The agency's mission was to provide a living arrangement so that the women and girls could bring their unborn children to healthy births and avoid the perceived need for an abortion. The agency was successful in assisting them to healthy births but difficult dilemmas occurred when the young mothers had to leave the facility two weeks after giving birth. There were often no good living solutions.

She found that all the women and girls were cut off from their families. The program taught them something about connecting by hosting quarterly reunions for former residents and their infants/children and family members. Those former residents who maintained contact in this way were less likely to become pregnant again without a long-term committed relationship with the father than those who didn't.

In families with rebellious kids discipline is not based on principle nor is it well thought through. *What happens as a result of irresponsible behavior with this parent depends more on the parent's mood at the time* rather than on appropriate guidelines or natural consequences of stepping out of bounds. For that reason consequences of behavior are not consistent in their intensity or predictability. The same irresponsible behavior may elicit a spanking or grounding at one time and no response at another.

CONFLICT   DISTANCE

JOHNNY'S PARENTS' ALTERNATING RELATIONSHIP POSTURES

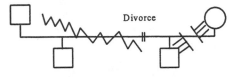

JOHNNY'S RELATIONSHIP WITH HIS PARENTS, CONFLICT WITH HIS FATHER, DISTANCE WITH HIS MOTHER

In addition to the parental focus drawn by younger children and teenagers with troubled behavior there may be a conflictual relationship pattern present. The whole thing may blow up into cutoff eventually. If the relationship difficulty can be addressed and put on a better basis, the behavior problem in the child will improve and then disappear, especially if the parents are working on their own relationship issues at the same time.

Kids who are cut off from their family will often try to create a substitute family in a cult or a gang. When interviewed, these kids consistently refer to their gang member friends as their family. Both gangs and cults are characterized by cutoff and drug use but the gangs take a violent posture to a degree unknown for the most part to the cults.

In working with young people as well as adults with conduct problems, Michael Sullivan has found that the behavior can be understood only in the context of the family relationships system. He found people in these families displayed a tremendous amount of "relationship intensity" with each other—that is, they invested a great amount of life energy in the family relationships. In addition, they showed three phases in their relationships with each other. These were:

1. Togetherness—with immature displays of affection, where a mother, for example, would refer to her incarcerated adult son as "baby boy."

2. Conflict—where agitated disagreement can involve excessive swearing and vulgarity, physical threats, destruction of property, or violence to persons.

3. Separation—a phase characterized by running away in response to a sense of being emotionally overcrowded or incarceration in which the parents and offspring, however physically distant, continue to think about each other.

Sullivan sees these relationship patterns not only in the nuclear families of the young people but also throughout their extended families. Where there are chronic conduct problems, he sees that patterns of instability such as multiple marriages, divorce, cutoff, poor employment histories and legal difficulties are common across the family network.

When Sullivan looked at juvenile offenders who went on to become adult offenders and compared them to those who did not, he found that "70% of the adult offending group had a cutoff with a parent compared to 5% of the non-offending group."

Irresponsible—or "conduct disordered," or "acting out," or "rebellious"—kids have an interesting relationship with society itself. They are certainly a part of society's problem. On the other hand, society seems to be egging them on, adding enormously to their problem, providing them with seemingly limitless opportunities for damaging, out of control, senseless actions. In this way society itself, to the extent that it is disorderly and involved in illegal activity, increases the problem of our kids. The kids, for their part, by acting out in public, become liabilities to society, actually deepening the regression. *They have literally taken their families' relationship problems to the streets.*

Society, on the other hand, does not really know what to do with kids whose emotion-based activities are getting out of control. Society may be adding to the problems they have in the ways it attempts to deal with them. We hear about people who come out of the penal system more hardened criminals than when they went in. Mr. Sullivan, studying the effects of societal intervention found that "juveniles who were made wards of the Department of Social Service and/or placed in residential facilities had the highest rate of adult recidivism of all." And the more intense the societal intervention the poorer was the long term outcome. Placement and incarceration were determined by the reactivity between the family and the court rather than by the facts of the case.

Ann Bunting, a psychotherapist and teacher of family systems theory, believes that constructive change in the prison system or in assisting offenders may be impossible because of the way the prison system and families interact. Families often define the prisoner as a victim of abuse by mental health professionals, society, and prison officials, while corrections personnel tend to characterize offenders as "sociopaths," blaming the families.

She sees these two positions as emotionally based, inhibiting contact between the corrections system and the family. The offender then undervalues the prison system, and overtly or covertly acts out against it. At the same time, the prisoner overvalues the family system overlooking the relationship difficulties that contributed to the acting out in the first place. They are reactivated upon release. If the two relationship systems could work together in constructive ways, rebellious people would automatically be held more accountable by both family and society. Family systems ideas could show the way in such an effort.

Irresponsibility may seem to be the norm—at least in some sectors of society. So parents themselves are put under subtle or overt pressure to think and behave irresponsibly themselves. It is difficult to hold on to their standards for what is acceptable behavior and what is not. If all the kids one knows are involved in drugs, parents may have a tendency to see drug use as not such a big deal.

If parents, keeping their principles in mind, can think things through all the way to clarity, they are able to end up in a very different place than where the societal regression is headed. This lack of fitting in with the world can be most difficult. But we as parents cannot really expect anything from society. We can say what we think, however. Responsible parents can define themselves differently—perhaps than anyone else they know—and can find a responsible stance. They can create a family unit with different expectations than many others who are caught up in the regression of the society at large—expectations based on their carefully thought-through principles.

Consistently responsible parents, attentive to their principles, their adult relationships, and connected to their youngsters, rear responsible children.

Emotional 5 Illness

Some problems show up in mood or thinking difficulties rather than in learning behaviors or use of substances. These are called emotional illnesses, mental illnesses, or brain disorders (the newest designation). It is not known what triggers these disorders, but there may be several avenues to them. Some being currently studied are genetic abnormalities, brain trauma, and biochemical or anatomic irregularities in the brain. Another pathway may at times have to do with anxiety in the family system. It is this latter, relationship trigger for mood and thinking problems that concerns us here. Although several triggers may be present in the same person, relationships play a key role, sometimes in bringing about symptoms, and often in exacerbating and keeping them alive over time.

When family anxiety gets high enough, over time its impact in one person, usually the focused one, can be serious. Specifically, the chemistry of the brain can be affected. Brain chemistry can disturb the sleep, the appetite, and the mood, leading to clusters of symptoms. Some of these clusters are: the various depressive disorders, obsessive-compulsive disorder, bipolar illness, anxiety syndromes such as panic disorder, and psychotic disorders such as schizophrenia. A great deal of research is going into finding the causes of these disorders. It may turn out that family anxiety is not one of the precipitating factors in some of these illnesses but, rather, they may begin from a genetic rearrangement, a biochemical lack or excess, or an anatomical malformation. On the other hand, it may yet turn out that family anxiety leads to chemical and anatomical endpoints such as these. *In any case, it is very probable that, at the very least, family anxiety, once the focus on the child with a problem gets going, greatly adds to the problem.*

Becky

Becky's family had gone through many changes. On the heels of a corporate buy-out, her father had lost his job. It took him a while to recover from the shock and then find another job. In the interim, the family finances became depleted, adding stress upon stress. Her mother worked as an office manager, keeping the family going, but she began to resent her new role as primary breadwinner when her husband showed so little initiative in moving on and finding another job. Their relationship, somewhat distant to begin with, deteriorated into intense distance and conflict. Becky, at sixteen, was the older of two girls. She tried to help the family by looking for cheaper living quarters for the family. After they moved into their new apartment, Becky became embarrassed to be around her more affluent friends. She spent almost all her spare time working at her fast food restaurant job.

As her parents' anxiety increased Becky lost her appetite and lost many pounds. Later, it became almost impossible for her to sleep as she worried about her parents' relationship, the family income, and what would happen to them all. Her mother had been worried about Becky for some time since her grades had dropped, and she looked too thin and not well. Becky's mother gave her some over-the-counter sleeping pills but they did not work. After several nights of almost no sleep, Becky began to hear voices in her head telling her to kill herself

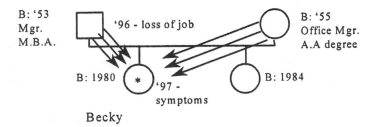

B: '53
Mgr.
M.B.A.

'96 - loss of job

B: '55
Office Mgr.
A.A degree

B: 1980   *   '97 -
symptoms

Becky

B: 1984

BECKY'S FAMILY DIAGRAM

and she spoke incoherently. At this point she was admitted to a hospital. With medication and understanding she improved and was then treated as an outpatient. The family relationships were explored over time. It was only when those relationships began to work a little better that she was able to go off her medication and thrive again.

One Parent's Efforts

Let's see what happened in another family. The mother describes what she experienced and how she thinks about it:

> "I have a daughter who has been diagnosed as suffering from bipolar (manic-depressive) disorder. During her childhood and early adolescent years, I did not see that she had any significant problems. When she was in high school, she seemed to need more direction from me. I spent more and more time discussing her problems with her and helping her solve them.

> "At the beginning of the second semester of her freshman year she became psychotic and had to leave school. I was stunned. In the five years after that incident I've come to have a way of thinking about 'mental illness.'

> "From infancy I had related to this daughter differently than to my other daughters. I worried about her and protected her from problems and disappointments that I feared she could not handle. At the same time I became more critical of her because she did not meet my expectations.

> "As a child, I was very important to my own mother. She suffered from both physical and psychiatric illness, and I spent a great deal of time helping her function. I believe that my need for her attention and approval drove my devotion to her well-being. I saw my mother as a burden and did not recognize my dependence on her. That dependence was transferred to my daughter. I responded to any distress in her as my distress. Her problems were my problems.

> "My daughter once described a psychotic state as an escape. To me that description is accurate. She becomes overwhelmed with others' expectations and does not think she has the ability to handle a problem, so she escapes. I have learned that when I am able to keep the focus off her and treat her as capable and separate from me, she is able to function as though that were the case."

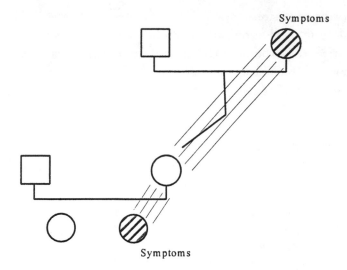

Symptoms

Symptoms

A SYMPTOMATIC CHILD
The lines illustrate how emotional intensity between generations is transmitted.

The great changes and chaotic conditions in the real world of societal regression directly affect families as did the unrest in the organization that led to Becky's father's loss of his position. Under these conditions, anxiety in some families goes sky high. This increases the incidence of symptoms including those of brain disorders (mental/emotional illness).

Also, the regressive conditions involved in managed care make it more difficult for a family to get appropriate treatment when needed. If a person is prescribed seven to fourteen days of rest and support in the hospital to regroup and go on, but the insurance company will grant only two or three days, it's more difficult to get started on the problem. In the regression there doesn't seem to be enough of anything to go around.

"Consumers" expect quick fixes or a program that will have the answers. Very few people seem to understand that the answers are within themselves and their family relationships. Almost no one is prepared to spend time, effort, and money exploring and then changing his or her own contribution to the family problem. In the long term, this is the only effective means of really improving the situation.

Psychotherapy is often ineffective because it is narrowly focused on "the patient" and pathology rather than looking more broadly for interaction problems in the family system and how they may affect the one with symptoms. Therapists lead clients through explorations of their weaknesses and bad feelings. Only a few therapist look for the strengths in the person, in the family, and in family interactions.

On the other hand, a psychotherapist, working from the Bowen theory and addressing the strength of the family (one or both of the parents), recognizes the family as the emotional unit and that the leaders of the family unit have the ability to change themselves. Unless they work on their relationship patterns there will be no changes in the weakest members.

Mary Goepfert, as a consultant in internal medicine at a large state hospital, wanted to try her hand at psychiatry. She found a woman on the back wards, where people were usually sent when all forms of treatment had failed. Dr. Goepfert worked with the woman's mother. When the mother was able to take a stand with the daughter and "not let her run her house with her weird behavior" the daughter started to improve. In time, the patient recovered completely. Ultimately she was discharged and functioned productively in her profession.

Parents who are able to think and act on the principles of family systems theory can begin to see the child's "illness" more as a symptom of the family anxiety rather than a category that sets the child in concrete, lowering expectations and limiting him or her for life. These parents are able to see themselves as different from the child and, with work, the personal boundaries in the family become better defined. These parents are able to think things through and define to others how they see things. That is, they have a more objective view of reality rather than simply a subjective one. Thus they can act more out of reason than simply emotion. They can also listen to their children. They are able to enlist a hand from "helpers" who can see the bigger picture and fresh possibilities, challenging or encouraging them to rise to a better level of functioning when they themselves have run out of steam. They can begin to see the problems of the child as different from their own. They can define objective reality as they see it, when appropriate. Though they respect a condition and whatever limitations or treatment it may impose, they allow themselves, in time, to think of the child as recovered. They make the effort to forget about the problem and see the child as normal.

Chronicity (long-term mental/emotional illness that does not respond to treatment, or responds only partially) occurs when the role of the family relationship problem is never understood or addressed adequately. Often the author has witnessed the intensity of the family emotional process seeming to overpower the effects of any medication tried. When the emotional process between the parents is addressed and the focus changed from the child to what is not working well between the parents, children often lose their symptoms and no longer need medications at all.

Physical Illness

Some children with mounting anxiety do not show disordered behavior, dependence on substances, or mental illness/brain disorder. Instead, in these children, anxiety leads to shutdown, malfunction, or overfunction of various body systems. It is possible that illnesses such as anorexia, overeating, inactivity, overactivity, accidents, asthma, allergies, diabetes, glandular disturbances (e.g., thyroid), decrease in antibody production with frequent infections, cancer, and many other illnesses may be shown at some time to have a direct connection to family anxiety settling in one member.

Shirley

Shirley's parents continued year after weary year in a state of anger that meant they did not speak to each other. After she began dating in her sophomore year in high school, Shirley suddenly lost her appetite. She ate very little. When she did eat, it was in tiny portions of only two or three foods. When she lost a great deal of weight her mother took her to her pediatrician, who asked Shirley to eat at least a minimal number of calories each day. Shirley promised she would, but did not. Her parents were very concerned. The more her mother worried the poorer Shirley's appetite became. The doctor asked her mother to bring her whatever she would eat. Her mother complied, but Shirley's weight continued to decline. The parents forgot their own angry relationship standoff in their anxiety about their daughter's condition.

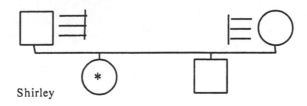

Shirley

Later

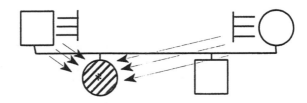

SHIRLEY'S FAMILY DIAGRAM

When Shirley's weight loss necessitated admission to a hospital, the family began to examine their relationships. Her mother, Mrs. A, carried a great deal of anger at her husband for various real and perceived slights and insults. Mr. A was distant and uninvolved, not seeming to understand or care about his wife's feelings. He became involved in the coaching, never missing a session. As her parents worked on their relationship with each other, Shirley's condition improved. As she began to eat and gain weight the family's anxiety lessened.

When Shirley's parents began to learn principles of family systems theory they could see how they were contributing to the problem. Their relationship intensities had made for constant anxiety in their home. The mother, previously intensely focused on Shirley, was able to get more of the focus on herself and her own marriage and work. Shirley continued to improve and ultimately made a complete recovery.

Medical professionals are usually narrowly focused on "the patient." They are almost never able to see the broader family relationship problem that may, at the very least, be adding to the patient's load of anxiety, bringing on or worsening the illness. In this way, they often join in the anxious family focus on the child and the problem, intensifying and emphasizing it. For the most part the medical profession does not have the training (nor sometimes the time or interest either) to assist the family toward strength through understanding its reciprocal relationship processes better.

Polly Caskie has studied physical illness through the lens of Bowen family systems theory. She emphasizes that there are knowable facts about any illness or symptom, based on scientific discovery, such as its incidence, its course, and possible outcomes. Everyone involved has a reaction to this knowledge, including the symptomatic child, the family members, and members of the health care system. Some people's reactions are so strong they aren't able to pay attention to or be interested in what is known. Other people are able to look for other facts in the situation, and make choices and decisions about what to do based more on the facts than on their feelings.

Dr. Caskie believes these emotional responses from parents, friends, community, and the health care system can influence the outcome of symptoms. For example, if the parent's reaction is to anxiously and fearfully focus on the child's health, though understandable in cases of life-threatening illness, this increases what the symptomatic child has to manage. But just as these automatic emotional reactions can have negative effects, more thoughtful responses, based on factual information, can help parents, family, and the health care system maintain a better perspective on the illness or symptoms. This perspective has calming, more positive effects on the symptomatic child. In short, if parents can learn to recognize and manage their own reactivity in the face of physical symptoms in a child (or anyone in the family for that matter), the child will have a better chance at recovery.

Family Violence

Pat

Whenever Pat's father reached a certain level of frustration he would begin loudly to find fault with Pat or whoever was in the room. At times he would "spank" Pat hard with a belt, as his father had him. Pat's mother was too afraid of her husband when he was upset to try to stop him. She thought about leaving him but had no idea how she and Pat would survive without the income of her husband. The quieter and more afraid of him she was, the more frustrated and upset he was. She had no idea that her own fear of, and lack of communication with, her husband was adding to the family problem.

Battered women often follow a pattern of behavior. The day after a battered and bruised woman comes in to the hospital, she is usually only too eager to tell her story—what happened, when and how. The second day of hospitalization, seeing her together with her husband, the husband tends to do all the talking. The woman is practically mute. It's remarkable. When asked how it makes him feel to have his wife sit there so quietly, he answers "furious." He is aware of his part in the relationship problem in the family but has no idea how to change it. She, too, is playing her part in intensifying the family problem but is totally unaware of how her mutely cringing in fear escalates the family anxiety.

In violent families there is enough anxious reactivity to go around, producing several "symptomatic" members when a parent lashes out in verbal, sexual, or physical abusiveness. Though the abusive parent

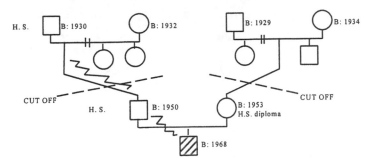

PAT'S FAMILY DIAGRAM

This diagram shows the conflict between Pat's father and grandfather showing up in Pat's generation as conflict between Pat and his father.

definitely has a symptom—his or her violent behavior—one or more children invariably develop symptoms in time.

Walter Howard Smith has made studies of many families with violence. He learned that though most people assume parents who injure their children with physical, emotional, and sexual violence do not care, this is not accurate. Observation of these relationships reveals that these parents care a great deal about their children—they demonstrate great concern about their welfare. In fact, the problem more nearly is that these parents care too much about their children. They are intensely emotionally involved in them.

Dr. Smith notices that actions of their children triggers strong emotional reactions in the parents. This reactivity can become so intense that parents have difficulty managing their behavior. The parents feel controlled by their children. "For example, when a daughter does not obey, a mother takes it personally and becomes enraged. She escalates her efforts. Her daughter resists. As these interactions occur, the emotional intensity builds. The daughter and mother equally threaten each other. From each perspective, their individual behavior makes sense. Both have good intentions. Both care. And both are trying to regulate and guide themselves in the relationship. This general pattern of interaction is predictable with child abuse and family violence."

Dr. Smith notices some predictable conditions when emotional investment by parents is too intense:

1. The intensity of parents' emotional investment in their children is related to the unresolved issues these parents have in their families of origin. The more parents have distanced from their families of origin as a way of managing conflicts and tensions the greater the investment parents have in their children.

2. Marital conflict is always present with child abuse. How parents perceive their children is shaped by the marriage. Some parents turn to their children for needs usually met in marriage. Others perceive their children as threats to the marriage. Other parents are divorced and isolated from all family supports, including their spouses.

3. How parents manage relationships in their families of origin and marriage has profound influence on the quality of relationships with their children. Ultimately, the quality of parents' caring for their children rests in the quality of other significant relationships in the lives of parents.

Douglas Murphy observes that "Children who have grown up in families where physical violence has occurred frequently experience difficulties with their own intimate adult relationships, as well as other areas of their adult functioning." The prevailing explanation emphasizes the learning and trauma involved in such families. Murphy believes, however, that learning and trauma have an effect in adult functioning, but they are not as important to the outcome in the adult's life as the patterns of relationship process in their nuclear and extended families.

He has seen children in some violent families maintaining better functioning by establishing relationships of their own with extended family members, such as a grandparent or aunt or cousin, or a significant adult outside of the family. Continued extended family connectedness will go a long way to neutralize the family violence the person grew up with.

Often, violent parents have grown up with some form of violence. If not, they are almost always cut off from their nuclear and extended families.

It is not always the parents who are violent. Sometimes kids become violent and abusive of each other or of parents. In this circumstance it is the parents' responsibility to stop the violence. In the short run whatever disciplinary and safety measures are needed must be thought through ahead of time and put in place. In the long term the violence will disappear if parents, the leaders of the family, will work on decreasing their own anxiety levels, and their reactivity within the family relationships, beginning with their own.

Violence can be seen as an outgrowth of the family emotional relationship process both of the nuclear family and of the generations of nuclear families. Unless someone learns how to interrupt his or her own emotional patterns the process can continue on and on as a multigenerational process. Usually when violence breaks out in a family there are several generations in the extended family that knew the pattern growing up. But this is not always the case. Families can be very innovative at times of unusual stress. They can "invent" violence in one generation.

Like other patterns of emotionally based behavior, violence and abuse are expected to increase at times of societal regression, both in the family and in society. Violence in society is one of the symptoms of the regression and can be seen as an indicator of the breakdown of the family. As the family disintegrates, intense violence can accompany that collapse, spilling out into streets and schools.

Parents Approaching Violence

Parents, trying to take the high road and encountering violence and abuse in their own families, understand that there are at least three areas for continued focus that are useful. Though the symptom needs to be attended to and contained, they will also want to take a look at the marriage posture(s) they have helped to create. They also will want to take many long looks at the generations of their own families. This will include looking at the relationships as well as whatever general facts can be ascertained about them. Since any outcome, including a symptom, is grounded in the generations of our own families, the better we understand our own families, their intensities and their emotional process (triggers, outcome, and process), the better we can understand the immediate problem we face and how to manage ourselves in it. In other words, as parents get the bigger picture, they can put the problem they face in context. Once they have the context better in mind, they start to develop ideas for how they themselves are contributing to the family intensity, what an interruption in the violent pattern would look and feel like and what it would take to make such a change.

Most families with a symptom of violence will want to engage a consultant in family theory to assist in their efforts to get things under control and then learn something about going on to a higher level of functioning.

Further, some families find community assists to be useful. These are sometimes most helpful to buy time for the family while it is in the process of improving its functioning. Families can plan for how to make the best use of these supports. Pat Hyland, consultant in family theory, along with others, has found that families are experts on their own angry and out-of-control members. She has found that she can assist them to think through what community aids they might need as they struggle with violence and other problems. Some of these invaluable helps have included mentors, arbitrators, and sitters, as well as classes to increase individual and family control. These measures can shorten hospital or correctional facility stays.

Adam

Hyland illustrates how this worked for one of her clients' family: Adam, age 14 and a high school freshman, was out of control. He was not obeying his parents and was not doing well in school. His parents were concerned he might be drinking and possibly using drugs. His younger sisters were afraid of and avoided their brother. He could often get angry and out of control, threatening his parents and others. He was hospitalized following an angry episode. He wanted to die and threatened to shoot himself. A brief hospitalization settled the immediate crisis, but more was needed. His father, age 70, had developed heart problems the year before. All family members were concerned that his health was deteriorating and that he could die at any time. Adam's mother was 44.

Over the last year the family had become increasingly isolated. Natural community support systems were put in place to support and stabilize Adam and his family. The support team included a local college student who would spend time with Adam three days per week, help him with homework, and provide companionship. They both enjoyed participating in and watching sports. The school counselor would clarify school assignments and be in weekly contact with Adam's mother. The parents would attend their church more regularly, and Adam would become more involved in youth activities. Adam discovered the associate youth minister could also play guitar and would give him lessons, something he had wanted for a long time. A neighbor offered Adam part-time work in his store. Adam now had his own spending money and wanted to use some of his money for clothes and other necessities. He took on a volunteer position helping younger children at a skating rink two hours a week, which seemed to do wonders for his self-esteem.

Family therapy helped the family improve communication and discuss openly their fears, anxieties, and plans. The father's younger sister and her family, who lived in a nearby town, became more involved and available as they were contacted and informed of current events. The sister's family had formerly felt cut off and not important. Both families benefited from the increasing contact. Regular meetings by the team were conducted, at first, weekly, and then less often. With this added support, Adam's life became more full and structured. His anger decreased and he returned to age appropriate functioning. Adam and his younger sisters now enjoyed a mutually satisfying relationship.

The intervention Hyland described is not necessarily typical of or limited to family systems thinkers, but is, rather, a relatively new and experimental way of lending a hand to families in order to avoid institutionalized care. Some of the factors that assisted Adam to higher functioning were from outside the family (community input). Do these help a family make necessary changes? Probably not, except in the sense that the assists can take pressures off an overburdened family while it is making needed improvements in the relationships with each other. To the extent that the extended family lent a hand, we are dealing directly with family systems ideas that always emphasize the importance of the wider family system in all its many functions.

As societal problems intensify, we are seeing more violence among children and adults alike. What do we do if we see actual or impending violence in our own family? Perhaps most importantly, families trying to change a violent pattern need to work toward as thorough an understanding as possible of the novel idea that the problem is not concerned merely with a "perpetrator" and a "victim." *A whole family system is involved and each member plays its part in the pattern.* Both nuclear and extended families as well as several generations of multi-generational emotional process have contributed as well. Each nuclear family in those generations brings its heritage from two sides but also acts as a unit itself in all its complexity and, at times, predictability. At the same time, any one person, by being a calm presence, staying connected with the symptomatic one, has the power to calm the emotional intensity that leads to violence.

What specific steps can be taken to calm the troubled waters of violence—the threats or acts against self or others?

1. Don't defensively blame the eruption on society—school, movies, friends, or TV. While they may all play a part, the family factor is far and a way more important. Either parent, by calming his or her own anxiety, and being more connected with the symptomatic one, has the power to make things better.

2. In the case of violent behavior, seek professional help. Run, don't walk to the nearest family systems trained therapist you can find. Hospitalization or incarceration may be temporarily needed, but they are only temporary solutions. Long-term change of any consequence will take place in the nuclear unit and will be the responsibility of the parents. The primary work will be done by them. Parents are the best coaches for children, not therapists. The child will change in response to the parents' better emotional functioning.

3. Parents are not to blame. It takes many generations of intensity to produce violence. However, either parent has the power to change his or her own reactions and connectedness in ways that will make a tremendous difference for the better.

Beyond the
Problem Focus

As we have seen, all the problem areas we have looked at in children are intensified, if not initiated by a parental focus. Although certain common problem areas have been selected, as far as is known, the general principles can be applied to many other problems of children. As the problem increases in severity, the family emotional focus becomes more anxious, intensifying the problem in an ever increasing spiral.

As the focus on the child increases there is a loss of focus on self by each parent. The parents' needs, interests, and adult relationships take a second place to those of the child. Curiously, this can make the marriage of the parents seem to function better or less well. Generally, however, when parental relationships don't get the attention they need and deserve, in time, they can begin to founder.

Sometimes parents involved in an intense child focus claim that their relationship is doing well, and if it were not for the child with a problem, the family would be just fine. However, experience shows that if it is only the child focus that has made these parents forget their unresolved conflicts, the success of the marriage is more apparent than real. Once they get the focus off the child, their relationship problems come to light and can then be observed and addressed.

People are more vulnerable to focus on problems in times of societal regression because of the greater amount of anxiety in the society and all its individuals. As anxiety mounts, vision becomes myopic.

Ability to see the bigger picture, or the complexities of a group, diminishes in most people.

Anxiety is on the increase, irresponsibility abounds, relationships break down and standards slip. Under these conditions, literature available to parents in popular magazines and books is strongly influenced by, if not a part of, the regressive trends. Traditional theory of the helping professions may have, in some important ways, added to the regression in society as well as to the problems for families rearing children. They do not know where to turn to find clear thinking. Many have no idea of how to begin to think about the problems in their own families.

Parents Refocusing

Some of the steps parents might take to work their way out of a problem focus would be:

- Observing self more—their own thinking, feeling, and behavior
- Taking the time and making the effort to think through their own principles as separate from the regression in society
- Attending to their own personal needs and interests more
- Attending to their own adult relationships so their lives are not totally absorbed by the symptom
- Seeing how the nuclear and extended family systems' emotional pressures play parts in producing the problem
- Seeing how they themselves play a part in the problem in the family, making appropriate adjustments in relationship stances and anxiety within self
- Not distancing from the child in an effort to not focus on the problem but maintain positive emotional contact with the child
- Working with the child around the problem in ways that are appropriate, based on facts and with as much calm thoughtfulness as possible.

If premises we have been holding are inadequate, how do we begin to think anew about human behavior and specifically human interactions in families? Clearly, a framework is needed—a theory that will provide a framework for thinking. If there is a way to think that more accurately describes how individuals and families interact with each other and with society then it could act as a set of principles for parents. Those principles could then guide behavior and interactions in relationships.

Bowen family systems theory has, for thousands of families, provided a superior framework upon which to anchor thinking about how families and the individuals in them interact at worst and at best. It provides a way to think beyond the individual and his/her problem. It encourages people toward clarity of thinking, leadership, and vision that can take self and the whole family group out of the morass of society in regression and on to a better level.

But one will never know personally whether a theoretical framework is true to life without getting some mastery of its ideas and practicing the principles in living relationships. A short summary of Bowen family theory follows, a kind of primer to act as a first step to take in understanding the theory. A primer is an entry—a door opening—on what becomes for serious students a very exciting and extremely meaningful lifelong effort.

Now, let's take that closer look at Bowen family systems theory itself, for only in taking the dual plunges of learning and application can one begin to understand its value and usefulness.

Part Two

How Successful Parents Think

A SYNOPSIS OF
BOWEN FAMILY SYSTEMS
THEORY FOR PARENTS

Families Are Systems

About Theory

It is difficult to think. It may be the hardest work the human has to do. It is lonely work and it takes a lot of energy. Because of that, many people rarely think a problem all the way through to a solution. However, when they step back, take a look, and start to think about the emotional process that is always happening in their families, they can make significant changes in the ways they interact with others. What they look at with the guidance of theory includes the pathways and patterns that anxiety takes, and their own contribution to both problems and possible solutions. Just looking at one's own system from as emotionally neutral a position as possible, of course, changes the one who does the looking. When one goes beyond looking and begins to make basic changes within one's self, it is noticed by the system. When that happens, of course, the whole system already is involved, for *when one person makes some basic changes, the whole system does.* That is when parents begin to see changes in the younger generation.

It is difficult to change one's way of thinking. Most of us are full of biases, prejudices, and other superficially examined beliefs that determine the course of our lives in ways we may not understand. Many of the ways we think may, as we have seen, be a part of the culture at large, and though these ways of thinking don't serve us well, they are so prevalent that they go unquestioned. The majority rules. Other guiding beliefs may have come down to us through our families implicitly or explicitly. Others may have been taught to us in school or other institutions. It is difficult to think at all, but to think through one's guiding principles and then challenge them is so hard that it probably will be accomplished only by very few.

It is even more difficult to *think systems*. That involves a change in the usual thought patterns for most of us, in ways for which we are not prepared at the onset. Most of us think "individual" by habit and by teaching. This is reinforced in almost all literature. It is cause-and-effect thinking that sees only a part of the problem. Thinking systems for most of us requires that we make a Herculean effort to try to see more of the players, patterns, and parameters than we are accustomed to looking at. Normally we are tied up in our own problem(s)—too aware of who is or was affecting us individually and how that affects us to get the bigger picture. When we can think more broadly, focusing on the system, a whole new world opens up. It becomes clear that people do not act in isolation but as elements of something much bigger—the system. How they think and act is for the most part, a function of the workings of that system. Now, to take that next step toward learning to think systems. For those who have made the effort it has been more than worth it, as they watch themselves and their whole families turn in a better direction.

Thinking Systems

If I think about my relationship with my mother, my father, my brother, and my sister and how they all affected me as a developing individual, I am thinking along the lines of a theory that sees the individual as the emotional unit. I am the center of the investigative universe. However if I am thinking about the family as the emotional unit, then I become interested not only in how all these people affected me, but also how I affected and affect them (most of the relational patterns are still going on), how they affected and affect each other emotionally, and how the triangles made up of individuals work to move anxiety among the individuals. Not only that, I will begin to see how the triangles in the extended families on both sides operate in anxious situations. Now I am beginning to think systems.

In thinking systems, one will try to see not only how one individual is being affected but also what the relationships are like between as many of the people in the family system as possible, and how anxiety passes between and among them. This is, of course, a very different problem than trying to take the measure of one person's problem. Sometimes managers can think systems, to a degree, at work, but upon arriving home, think more "individual."

Unlike quick fixes, easy answers, and methodologies, family systems theory shows a broader way of thinking about any situation. In contrast, if one learns a method or technique for doing something or fixing something, it will apply to only a limited number of situations. Endless numbers of methods will have to be learned in order to cover all the possible situations. Alternatively, if one has a theory that is true to life, it will point the way in any possible situation. This is why theory is so important. Thus, although theory may require some effort in learning to think in a different way, once mastered, it is invaluable, for it will "show the way out" in any circumstance of life.

Many, if not most of the serious dilemmas of our lives have to do with relationships and relationship systems, either in our families or workplaces. When emotional intensity mounts in a relationship system, energy and time are drained from more productive life pursuits. If one can go to a set of principles that will not only help to delineate the problem but also show how to think about it and what steps to take to start to solve it, one has an advantage that, clearly, most people do not.

Although it may be for the few, for those people clinical experience shows that their relationships, and therefore their families and offspring, do better in *many* ways. Perhaps those few can show the way for others eventually, if only in rearing their children in a little better way than they would have otherwise.

During times of societal regression all groups of people have a more difficult time—families, workplaces, and organizations. Families dissolve with greater frequency. Because of workplace and economic chaos it is more difficult for the family to exist financially, so parents may have less time and energy for children than they really need. Having lost sight of principles, many act less responsibly in the parental role.

If parents think systems, they can learn to recognize all the difficulties out there, the ones within the self and the ones in their families, and know the difference. They can see the system as well as any individual in it, with its problems and their own. They can see their personal strengths and those in their families and begin to operate from that perspective. They can become more sure of their guiding principles and constantly make the daily effort it takes to live within them. They can define their principles to themselves and their children and know that, even when it seems they are not, they are making a difference. Often they'll see it much later. But there are encouraging signs of progress all along the way.

A New Way to Think

As Bowen designed it, family systems theory has eight formal concepts.

CONCEPT 1: TRIANGLES *The triangle is the most stable small unit of emotional systems.* In groups of people anxiety routes itself around this "molecule" of human interaction and of society itself. When two people have a problem interacting, a third will often be attracted or drawn in by the original twosome. The focus on a child is an example of a triangle, where parents, ignoring their original problem, allow the anxiety generated by its lack of resolution to become directed at a child. In a patterned way, the family anxiety then flows automatically toward the child. "Triangling" can result in insiders and outsiders, with two agreeing the other is "the problem" or "wrong."

CONCEPT 2: SCALE OF DIFFERENTIATION OF SELF The idea of differentiation of self is a fascinating, challenging, and most inspiring concept for those who take it on. *The scale of differentiation of self refers to a theoretical scale that separates people along a continuum of zero to one hundred according to their ability to adapt over a lifetime.* More differentiated people do well in most areas. Less differentiated people do less well. *The basic reason for this concerns how they function emotionally in relationships, derived from years of functioning in their families of origin, their formative relationship system.* This can be estimated roughly but never accurately measured, since that would involve looking at an entire lifetime.

How we function in relationships actually affects the brain and how it handles thinking and emotions. At the higher end of the scale there is more choice between the intellectual system and the emotional/feeling system and at the lower end, little or none. Because of this ability to choose thinking or feeling, thinking at the high end of the scale is clearer. For this reason *their clarity on what they think—their beliefs—can act as an inner guidance system that is available to them, made up of principles.*

The way we function in relationships is built into us by the time we leave home and determines our comfort in, dependence on, and success in relationships. At the higher end of the scale people are freer from emotionally fusing into relationships, and they are more comfortable and successful. This relationship functioning success promotes success in other areas of life also—vocational, social, mental/emotional/brain functioning, and physical health. People higher on the scale have more individuality (basic self) and less togetherness (tendency to fuse into relationships).

At lower ends the relationship fusions make for less satisfaction and stability. Anxiety at the lower end of the scale is higher and functioning is lower in all areas (social, mental/emotional/brain, physical).

CONCEPT 3: NUCLEAR FAMILY EMOTIONAL SYSTEM *The nuclear family as an emotional unit, rather than the individual, is the idea most fundamental to all the other concepts and the idea that changes the way one thinks.*

When people live together in a family they tend to pass anxiety from one person to another in the family. *When anxiety automatically moves in relationship systems it often does so in stereotyped ways* that become relationship "postures" or "patterns" among the two or three people involved. These specific patterns that arise are
- conflict
- distance
- overfunctioning/underfunctioning reciprocity
- triangling

Each is adopted to manage the anxiety. When used excessively and habitually, they also give rise to anxiety.

CONCEPT 4: MULTIGENERATIONAL EMOTIONAL SYSTEM *Not only does anxiety move between members in a nuclear family, it also travels across the generations.* When the generations of a family are studied in the framework of family systems theory, the importance of movement of emotionality through the generations can be seen in family stressors, themes, and differences in functioning in different branches of a family.

CONCEPT 5: FAMILY PROJECTION PROCESS Not everyone in a nuclear family has the same level of differentiation even though the two parents are theoretically at the same level. *The family emotional process, through relationship fusions, affects some of the offspring more than others.* In this way anxiety is off-loaded to the children in a family in differing amounts, some getting less focus and anxiety, some more. This anxiety seems to be taken on by the child more or less permanently. For this reason the degrees of differentiation of self of siblings (and thus, their lives) may look very different.

CONCEPT 6: SIBLING POSITION Personality has many determinants. One of those, delineated by the important research efforts of Dr. Walter Toman, is *sibling position as described by both age rank and gender configuration within the family.* He showed how the nature of relationships and their challenges, as well as their strengths, are strongly affected by the sibling positions of the people involved.

CONCEPT 7: CUTOFF *The most extreme form of distance in relationships is called cutoff.* Cutoff occurs when people significant to one another discontinue contact with one another. It produces extreme effects in the form of poor relationships in other areas of life. It also leads to other symptoms, emotional, physical, or social. Cutoff is produced by extreme emotional intensity that one or both parties ultimately find intolerable.

CONCEPT 8: SOCIETAL EMOTIONAL PROCESS Sometimes called societal regression, this concept refers to the *periods of chaos, disorderliness, and irresponsibility that occur in society at large at times of greater anxiety.* It is unclear what triggers the societal anxiety that leads to periods of regression—many have been suggested such as: over-population, weapon threats, lack of leadership, economic threat, and decreasing availability of land and other resources. These may all have the common denominator of threat to survival.

These eight concepts comprise the formal theory as described by Bowen. Actually, they are only the beginning of Bowen theory. Concepts such as individuality/togetherness, thinking systems, natural systems (how much like other species are the emotional parts of the human brain and behavior), spirituality, and anxiety itself are considered in detail by those who think by principles of Bowen family systems theory and in reality become a part of the theory as it is already expanding and being refined.

The Idea That Changes Everything

Seeing the family rather than the individual as the emotional unit is an idea that changes the way one sees everything. For most of us, seeing the group as the unit is a radically different way to think. Getting one's head around this idea carries a tremendous impact for thinking, feeling, and moving in the world. In order to begin to grasp the idea of the family as the unit we must learn to *think systems.* What does that mean and how do we do it?

The whole of Bowen family systems theory is about "systems" and how people interact emotionally in them. What is a system? *Simply put, a system is a group of individuals who together form an identifiable unit. This unit comes about by simply living and spending time together.* Anxiety is passed among individuals in stereotypical patterns. One can tell who is in the group and who is not. Reading about someone outside one's family having an affair, for example, is quite different from learning about an affair from one's spouse!

More specifically, this theory concerns itself with *natural systems.* Natural systems no doubt behave like other systems (such as the stars and planets, the weather, or the atoms in a molecule) in many regards. But living natural systems are unlike physical or many other non-living systems we might think of. Since they are living systems, they behave differently from other systems—they are more open-ended and thus less predictable. It is living, or natural systems with which Bowen theory is concerned.

The human family as a natural system is like other natural systems in some important ways. Michael and Kathleen Kerr have studied research of species such as the naked mole rat and chimpanzees and shown how many similarities there are in the emotional systems of human families and of other species.

There are also some important differences. The human cerebral cortex, larger and more developed in areas such as speech and abstract thinking, gives human families capabilities that other systems do not have. We, for example, can look at ourselves and try to be less the victim of automatic responses in relationships. We can observe scientifically—objectively—for factual information and then make adjustments in ourselves that will affect the system based on that knowledge.

In a family there are many relationships between and among individuals. Anxiety and other emotions get processed in these relationships, moving around, among, and between the individuals in the family. In fact, one could draw a circle around the group, like a cell wall (see figure 7).

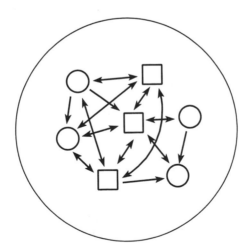

FIGURE 7

Within the circle, or wall, is contained the emotional unit, the system with all its relationships—all its fusions of selfs and constantly circuiting emotions. That sense of the larger group as the emotional unit rather than the individual is—for most people—the fundamentally new idea that changes the way they think.

If the group is seen as the emotional unit it is impossible to understand the individual except in terms of that group. The individual now is seen as a fragment of something much larger—the original family. Like it or not, one is and always will be, in some sense, a part of that larger whole. This means that in order to understand myself I have to understand as much as I can about how my family formed an emotional system. I will need to see how the relationships in my family meshed and interacted over time in rather predictable ways and how different people in the family, including myself, fit into that larger whole. That knowledge will give me a more accurate picture of myself than I could obtain in any other way.

For example, when I attempt to observe my family and watch how anxiety moves and how these patterns are repeated, I find out how I, myself, fit into it. Not only *am* I my family in some important ways, but I am also the unique fit that I had and still have emotionally with that group. *That is, I related with all the individuals in the group in my own way that was a little different than it was for anyone else in the family.* There was only one oldest daughter, one youngest son, or any other position one can name. Each was in an emotionally different position from the others. Each one received a bit different amount of family anxiety and so ended up in a little different place on the scale of differentiation, with a little more or less fusion with the others in the family, and thus with a different degree of basic self. So each self is different and the very differences themselves are derived from the repetitive emotional experiences of that self within the emotional unit—the family system.

Even the self—the guiding center of the individual—is defined in terms of relationships. How much autonomy, how much neediness in relationships, what emotional patterns one is most apt to fall into are all laid out during the many years of ingraining in that original family. All this, for a systems thinker, is the basis for success, for the ability to adapt in relationships and in life in general.

Now we can begin to see how grasping the fundamental idea of the family as the emotional unit changes the way one thinks about and approaches everything about the human phenomenon. How does it change our approach to child rearing? Does it contribute to our becoming more responsible, effective parents in the unpredictable world in which we now live?

Children develop in the emotional unit (system) called the family, and become like it in some ways, reflecting its strengths and weaknesses. That is, we all take on some of the strengths of our parents—their ability to be calm when others are upset, for example, or their charm or love of fun. We also take on parents' weaknesses to some degree—for example, their tempers, tendencies to worry, or short-sighted impulsiveness.

Children not only take on characteristics and tendencies from their families, they also develop their own unique sets of characteristics over time as a consequence of being in their particular positions in that family. For example, a child might be repeatedly frustrated in his or her family relationship position. Rather than taking on the characteristic of being easily frustrated directly from a parent, it is developed from constant practice in a particular relationship position in the group.

Yet, children also become individuals, not merely reactive, but *differentiating* to some degree from the group they grow up in. This ability to be, to some extent, outside the emotional system, to keep a neutral part of self that does not participate in the family intensities is an asset that can lead to relationship as well as other kinds of success. Most families automatically press the offspring to become pretty much as they themselves are, to fulfill their own needs for relationship. Some higher-functioning families are able to see the difference between their own (parental) relationship problem and that of their children, allowing everyone better boundaries and more emotional room.

While important attention is now being paid to the "village" in which children grow up, not enough is widely understood about the importance and workings of the family system in which they develop. But that family group with all of its intricate interactions will no doubt prove to be an overwhelmingly more important factor in how they turn out as adults. Too, the society itself has almost no chance of recovery if the basic unit of that society, the family, is not alive and functioning well.

10
Anxiety and
Its Crucial Effects

A part of being human is *emotional reactivity*. It is both an asset and a liability. As an asset, emotional reactivity enables us to see an oncoming car in the same lane and swerve out of the way. When the house catches on fire it enables the blood pressure and heart rate to rise, so that more blood gets to the brain enabling it to figure out better and faster how to escape or extinguish the fire.

In relationships, too, emotional reactivity allows courtship to take place, enabling relationships to flourish and become durable. It helps mothers to withstand wakeful nights with newborn infants. It also helps couples stay together, cooperating and supporting each other when their lives are filled with tremendous numbers of challenges and too much stress.

At the same time, emotional reactivity—as anxiety—can also be a liability. In relationships, for example, as we have seen, people regularly take on the anxiety of the other, just by being around each other.

If Dad, stressed by freeway driving, comes in the room in a bad mood, Mom, just by being around him, takes on some of Dad's frustrations and anxiety (see figure 8).

FIGURE 8

For simplicity, let us refer to any intense negative emotion as anxiety. It may be depression, frustration, or any one of a number of descriptions—at base all these may be considered anxiety. Unless medication is needed for specific symptoms it may be unnecessary to define anxiety further. Some intense positive emotions, such as extreme euphoria, are also, at base, anxiety.

What is anxiety? Traditionally, anxiety has been defined as a reaction to a threat or perceived threat. However, anxiety can be said to exist any time there is heightened emotional reactivity in an individual or in a group. Most commonly that reactivity will be elicited whenever there is a threat or a perception of a threat. But sometimes anxiety just moves from one to another without any threat perception. When Dad's anxiety goes up on the freeway he is under no threat—he simply wants to get home after a long day and is prevented by complicated traffic patterns and rude drivers from doing so efficiently. Much of the anxiety we experience today is of this nature—no real threat exists and we know it, but the frustrations and excessive sensory input of our complicated society raise the anxiety level all the same, resulting in heightened reactivity. Much anxiety of this daily kind recurs and takes a while to dissipate. It can be called *acute anxiety*—the insults and jabs that we take on a daily basis. Some of these acute stressors are small, like the freeway. Others are enormous, like the loss of a job or even the loss of a person from the family system.

Chronic anxiety is more of a background level of anxiety that people carry with them as a consequence of growing up in a family that carried in it a certain ambient level of anxiety most of the time. The nervous system probably absorbs this reactivity at a certain level, or pitch, while we are growing up and then keeps it going whether or not it is needed or appropriate for the life circumstances. Added to that personal level is the level that continuously circulates within the family we grew up in, affecting each of its members at all times. Each of us operates against a continuing hum, or in some cases, roar, of these two types of chronic stress or anxiety. This anxiety is not associated with threat perception; it simply is, in the family units, circuiting unceasingly within, between, and among its members.

Anxiety is additive, so that if one has a certain amount of background anxiety going all the time, and then added to that is freeway driving frustration, and added to that is a good and trusted friend moving far away, and added to all that is a spouse losing a job, it is easy to see how one's anxieties can add up to overload. Stress researchers Holmes and Rahe found that some stressors are more important than others and ranked them in order of importance; that is, death of a spouse, divorce, moving, and so forth. If people experience more than a certain number of the stressors in a period of time, they are likely to become physically or emotionally ill.

Nodal Events and Shock Waves

Some stressors are more difficult to categorize. They start out as acute, beginning at a definite point in time, but they become chronic. That is, the physical or other consequences of the stressor go on and on in time. Further, these stressors affect the entire family system in many if not all of its living generations. These are so important they are given a special name—*nodal events.* They are most often triggered when someone leaves (through death or divorce) or enters (by birth, adoption, or marriage) a family system. Other occurrences, however, can be important enough to qualify as nodal events with all the ensuing family fallout that implies.

When a nodal event occurs, the stress of it may affect not only the nuclear family of the person directly involved, but also other individuals in related families and different generations. In this way, important deaths can carry with them a "shock wave" effect throughout the extended family.

Bowen described it as follows: "It occurs most often after the death of a significant family member, but it can be almost as severe after a threatened death. An example was a grandmother in her early sixties who had a radical mastectomy for cancer. Within the following two years, there was a chain of serious reactions in her children and their families. One son began drinking for the first time in his life, the wife of another son had a serious depression, a daughter's husband failed in business, and another daughter's children became involved in automobile accidents and delinquency. Some symptoms were continuing five years later when the grandmother's cancer was pronounced cured."

The stress response of humans is interesting and complex. And different kinds of stressors induce different chemical responses in the body. For example, with the simple reactivity of courtship one set of neuroendocrine hormones comes into play. With long-term close connectedness, another. Still another set is elicited with childbirth. These would be experienced as positive emotions and not commonly thought of as anxious. However, in courtship the reactivity between people is intense and can still be experienced physically as stressful. In the same way the rapidly changing hormonal levels can be extremely stressful to a new mother.

Anxiety, with its negative feeling tone, calls forth yet another set of hormones. Its complicated hormonal stimulus-response pathways and networks are more commonly associated with the stress response. The *acute* stress response centers around the inside cells of the adrenal gland called the medulla. These cells, in an emergency or perceived emergency, secrete adrenaline in a complex chain of hormonal events that elevates blood pressure, heart rate, and breathing, readying the muscles and brain to respond to the emergency. The reactivity of *chronic* anxiety elicits a whole circuit of hormones involving secretions of the adrenal cortex, the outside shell of the gland. It secretes cortisone and related hormones. If stressors continue over time (different times in different people), there are many adverse physical and emotional effects. One of these is that the human antibody response declines so that the individual becomes vulnerable to infections.

When stressed optimally, humans think better, respond creatively, and experience life as satisfying. In other words, no stress at all is experienced as a boring life and that situation in itself can constitute a stress. But just the right amount of challenge, with the external and internal resources to meet it with some success, is experienced as exciting and fulfilling. New research on aging suggests that this promotes the brain's health and protects it against dementia.

When stressed beyond that optimal point, sleep quality declines and quantity declines or increases, appetite can become voracious or fall off, energy becomes depleted or surges into hyperactivity, and the mood may become negative or excessively euphoric. With chronic stress, reliable thinking declines and emotionally-based reactivity (including obsessive and worried thinking) increases. Behavior based on this reactivity can reflect bad judgment and invite consequences that are disastrous, in both the short and long term.

When stressed beyond an optimal point, the organism has three choices. The adrenal medulla, secreting adrenaline, readies the organism for the well known and described "fight or flight" responses. Ready for a fight, the organism becomes angry and threatening, often inappropriately so. If one decides that flight is the correct response one will leave the situation entirely. Either may be appropriate in the short term. Put into use over the long term, though, the personality or relationship becomes one of conflict (fight) or distance (flight).

Another type of response to chronic stress has the organism giving up and shutting down in a "freeze" response. In this strategy the organism "plays dead" in the hope of not being discovered. Physiology may actually close down as the breathing tubes do in asthma.

Lilian Rosenbaum, studying stress and reactivity in humans, believes that family relationship patterns can affect brain function. She observes that "The amygdala in the limbic system—the emotional part of the brain—affects anxiety. The amygdala and the hippocampus can be damaged by stress from a variety of sources including family, extreme social conditions like war, and by some prescribed drugs such as steroids that affect cortisol level." Cortisol levels correlate generally with stress levels.

Increasing anxiety has effects on relationships as well as individuals. Under the effects of anxiety, emotionally based patterns of relationship behavior intensify. People do more of what they always have done; it would take a lot of thought to do anything differently. That is, they fight (engage in conflict), flee (distance themselves), cut off entirely, overfunction/underfunction (dominate other or subordinate to other), or they focus their anxiety on a child (triangle). These postures, while mitigating anxiety for the short term, will add to it over the long haul.

Tessa Smith, in her work with marmosets, showed how relationship postures can actually add to the stress for individuals. She discovered that if the animals merely watch others fighting they show internal distress by secreting the stress hormones (detected in the urine). On the other hand, Smith found that relationships also mitigated stress for individual animals. If they stressed the animals by putting them in an unfamiliar environment, the experienced stress was decreased by putting their mates or siblings in the environment with them.

Most stressors, however, can be met by thinking about the situation until the right response becomes clear and then taking the appropriate action. When overwhelmed by several stressors, one can usually prioritize and deal with them in a thinking manner, one at a time, instead of staying overwhelmed, which can lead to inaction or inappropriate action and eventual symptoms. When one can get to some degree of emotional calm, one's thinking, decision-making, and behavior is more based in reason and logic. Under those circumstances long and short term outcomes are better.

Thinking not only helps us get to solutions of problems but *activity of the thinking part of the brain actually has an inhibiting effect on the emotional part of the brain.* This calming effect further supports reliable thinking.

It is very hard to think logically or creatively in the presence of anxiety, especially since thinking is perhaps the most difficult work we have to do under any circumstances. For that reason thinking is reserved, too often, for the last resort—if we get to it at all!

People around us (in our families, workplaces) will become reactive—emotionally intense, or anxious—from time to time, and the nature of relationships dictates that each of us has a tendency to take on the reactivity of the other. So relationships themselves become an important source of anxiety. *To some degree, however, we have choices involving whether to take on the other's anxiety or not.* If one is trying to respond thoughtfully to an anxious other, an attempt can be made to refrain from absorbing the anxiety of the other. Staying in calm emotional and intellectual contact with that other person can actually push up relationship functioning for the individual just as working out with weights improves the functioning of muscles over time.

Bonnie Sobel, a family systems theory psychotherapist, in teaching stress management, emphasizes that stress is not all bad. It can bring out the best in us. She looks at many different kinds of stressors, including physical, emotional, social, environmental, cognitive, and, especially, relationship stress. She sees the best stress management tools as being a healthful lifestyle and knowing one's own patterns of reactions. Sobel teaches deep abdominal breathing and brain exercises to enhance relaxation and attentional focus. These can be increased when people are faced with times of special stress such as at examination time, in relationship conflicts, or at times of rapid change in the family.

It must be remembered, though, when working with children, that they are merely the symptom-bearers of the family. If the parents do not work on themselves and their relationship patterns, symptoms will return or anxiety will produce symptoms in someone else.

By being aware of anxiety and its effects in self, in families, and in society, parents are in a better position to manage themselves in a manner that will, to some extent at least, deal more positively with the anxiety over time.

In just taking the observing position in a system, one can, in addition to learning a lot, sometimes be a little more outside the anxiety. One person getting a little more "out" has a beneficial effect on the whole group. Learning about the effects and management of anxiety in self so as to always be in the process of becoming less and less reactive to others and more thoughtful in one's responses takes relationship functioning to a better level.

The Family as an Emotional Unit —Reactivity in Action

The nuclear family can be seen as an emotional unit in many different ways. One way to see it is to notice how anxiety travels around the unit. Raise the anxiety in the group enough, and the relationships will become disturbed. At some point, the people in the family will start one or more of the following behaviors, also called patterns or postures: They will argue and fight with each other (conflict), move away from each other (distance), get bossy and overbearing (overfunctioning), or react to overfunctioning by being docile and easily led (underfunctioning), or involve a third person in one-to-one interactions (focus on child, or triangling). Originally, Bowen called the overfunctioning/underfunctioning reciprocity the dysfunctional spouse posture (the underfunctioner was the symptomatic spouse). He originally named the pattern of spouses triangling in a child, the symptomatic or focused child.

Parents are interested in understanding how it is that a symptom develops in a child based on family interactions. Yes, a *symptom*. Even the most dire "diseases" can be properly referred to as a symptom when thinking systems. Thinking of a child in trouble as carrying the family anxiety in his or her problem—that is, as an outgrowth of the family emotional system—gives a more accurate picture of what is going on in the family than focusing on a dire *diagnosis* and all that that implies about the individual as the problem. We saw in Chapter 2 how children develop (or increase) their symptoms, out of family anxiety.

If and when anxiety, with its attendant reactivity, gets going in a family and most of the anxiety ends up in a child, so that the child becomes symptomatic, we usually find that the parents are involved in some degree of child focus. In addition, parents can take any one of four other anxious postures toward a child. We will go into them all. But where there is a symptom in a child, the child focus is always present to some extent. So let's first review the child focus first before going on to the other relationship postures found between parents and their children.

The Child Focus

If the adults in a family do not solve their relationship or other anxieties as they come along, they will very often begin to focus on something that they perceive to be wrong with one of their children. Anxiety travels among people in a nuclear unit; therefore, if a worried focus on a child or children continues over a significant amount of time, the anxiety will come to rest in that child (see figure 9).

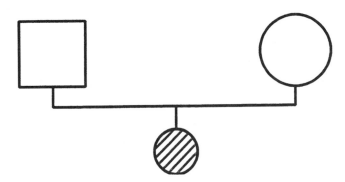

FIGURE 9

What happens to a person who is the object of worry? He or she gets anxious. If the person is a child, it is as if the child takes on the anxiety of the parents. Then, because of the effects of increased anxiety within, the child does less well—the problem automatically intensifies. That is, the original problem the parents worried about (bad grades, difficult breathing, lying, irresponsibility, or any one of a hundred others) worsens. The parents feel fine (except for the worry about the child) and often their relationship appears to be doing well, but the child neither feels nor does well. He or she comes to be seen as "the one with the problem" (see figure 10).

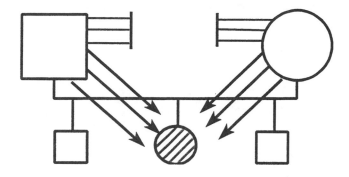

FIGURE 10

The more the parents worry, the more anxiety goes into the child. The more that anxiety lands in the child, the worse the child does with whatever the problem may be.

If it is suggested, on an initial visit about a child, "Worrying about your children is hostile behavior. Why be hostile to your children?" This usually elicits shock. "How can I not worry about my child who is not doing well?"

"I don't know, but if someone worried about you all the time what would it do to you? How would you feel? Could you succeed if worried about all the time? What would it do to your self-confidence?"

Often the parent will then tell about a parent of his or her own who actually did worry about him or her a lot. They remember what it did to his or her own functioning. Not meaning to replicate a problem, the parent has, nonetheless, because of the way anxiety automatically passes from parents to children through the generations (see figure 11, on the next page).

Further, when parents realize that displaced anxiety is making them feel better at the expense of their child, they are usually eager to take a look at their behavior. Once parents can look at their anxious worried relationship posture and the effect it may be having becomes apparent, the next part of their work can begin. How to change it?

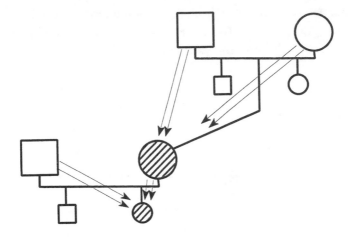

FIGURE 11

Changing a worried focus is no easier and no harder than turning it from the child to the self, observing what is there, and then finding a way to do that part of one's emotional functioning differently.

Many parents have found that when they were able to discontinue the worried focus on their children the problem in the child disappeared. Some continued to work on themselves in other ways since the unresolved marital problem usually becomes apparent after the focus comes off the child.

The child focus is one form that triangling in a family group can take. Murray Bowen describes triangles as follows: "There is a definite, predictable chain of 'moves' or maneuvers that occur in any three-person emotional system. The intensity of the moves depends on the importance of the people to each other, and the amount of tension in the system. It occurs among any three people in meaningful emotional contact, including social and work systems. It is most intense in the father-mother-child triangle in a family."

At the present time there is an intensified focus on children in our society. If you want to get a bill through Congress, pin it to children in some way. If you want to raise a lot of money, ask for it in the name of a cause for children. Is this "child focus" coming out of the regression? If society at large works anything like the families it is made up of, then an educated guess would have the child focus in society originating in society's intense anxiety and many unsolved problems.

When parents can contain their own anxiety and process it within the self and adult relationships, children will automatically do better.

Although child focus is invariably present where children are having problems, there may be varying degrees of the other relationship patterns or postures also. Let us see how they play out in parent/offspring relationships.

Conflict

Conflict between parents and their offspring can get started in several ways. Caught in a focus, a child may become mad and fight back. Or, conflicted parents may turn on one or more children with the same kind of intensity they generate in each other. Watching conflicted parents, a child may simply "do likewise," spewing the language and behavior of their conflict back at them.

Conflict is the "fight" emotion of the animal world. *It can take the form of criticism or any other kind of thinking that projects the problem on to the other. Its inflammatory invectives usually begin with "You——."*

Parents and children caught in conflicted postures become as intense, unreasonable, and illogical as do spouses in the same situation. A common conflict seen in consultation is the high achieving father whose son (or daughter) doesn't quite measure up. The son may be underachieving, or simply see different goals for himself than his father does.

MR. C Mr. C was embarrassed by his son's seeming lack of caring about his schoolwork. As Bill's grades fell, Mr. C called him lazy, stupid, and irresponsible. "How will you ever amount to anything in the world with this kind of attitude toward your schoolwork?" Mr. C himself had almost a perfect school record. It had not even occurred to him and his wife that one of their children might achieve any less. The more his dad accused him, the worse Bill felt. The worse he felt, the less work he did, and the lower his grades fell. He in turn accused and criticized his father of not caring about him and being a workaholic, calling him a jerk. Little did Mr. C know that when he accused, blamed, and criticized, his son actually believed all the names his father called him. So if his father called him stupid, Bill came to think of himself as stupid. Of course if one thinks of oneself as stupid one will not learn readily or pay much attention to what is going on in school.

In conflict, as in the child focus, the focus is so much on the other that, although either has the power to stop the fighting, neither is looking to see what he/she can do differently. If a parent can do that, however, things change dramatically and the conflict is over.

In consultation, Mr. C began to back off, placing more of his energy and focus on his own life and relationship with his wife. He learned that indeed he was a workaholic. This was related to the fact that his relationship with his wife had never worked very well, making time at work seem more attractive than time at home. He was not born a workaholic. He became one in his marriage relationship, seeking to escape what he perceived as the domination of his wife. He did not understand, nor have any way to think about changing, his own contribution to that pattern. She tended to be the dominant one, and he, the submissive one. Often, tiring of their respective relationship roles, they would break out into open conflict.

As he understood his roles in the family relationship system better, Mr. C worked to become more of a self in the relationship with his wife. He found more energy to do many things he had wanted to. Life became more interesting and exciting. He was able to get more work done in a shorter time. His relationship with his wife flourished in his new determination to keep the focus on how he could manage his emotions differently in the relationship. After she recovered from the shock of the changes in her husband, she began to adjust to having a responsive person around instead of a passive "no-self." Of course this meant she had to deal with him more. But, in time, both of them described the relationship as working better than it ever had.

From this position Mr. C could relate to his son a little more calmly and objectively. He realized that, although his family of origin had actually been rather peaceful, what conflict there was had centered around him. He had been in conflict not only with his father, but also with several of his siblings. Changing the pattern would have to begin there. He worked hard to relate to his father and siblings. As he did so, the name-calling and criticism of Bill stopped. He defined himself but did not try to define Bill's life or behavior. He began to "lend a hand" emotionally to Bill whenever it seemed needed. Eventually Bill accepted his dad's invitations for various activities.

The change in Bill was rapid and dramatic. He began to achieve. Old friends were dropped and new ones appeared. He began to take his schoolwork seriously. His life course was now headed in a very different direction. Later he became more of a leader. He even circled back to some of his old friends, showing some of them a better direction.

Distance

Tired of fighting (or other relationship intensity), any pair, including parents and children, may distance themselves from each other. Let's watch it in the D family.

MS. D. Linda D was unhappy following her divorce. She felt her life was over and she was just going through the motions. She had no energy to face the daily struggle to make a living and less to face her two teenagers at the end of the day. The last thing she wanted to do was to take out her bad feelings on her kids. But she felt so very bad that again and again she found herself doing just that—she seemed to have no control. Fifteen-year-old Susan handled the intensity by distancing, locking herself in her room and hanging out with a circle of friends of whose behavior her mother did not approve. Her choice of friends intensified her mother's unhappiness. But the distance was not altogether unfamiliar. As a teenager she herself had spent a lot of time in her room. And, on reflection she realized the distance from her own family had become more intense as an adult.

In consultation, as she reestablished contact with her parents and brother she began to feel some semblance of emotional stability beginning to assert itself. This groundedness helped her to reach out and establish a new system of friends. She had more energy and less anxiety. She could be more friendly with her children. Susan had less and less need to be in her room. She and her mother even discovered they enjoyed shopping and going to movies together.

Distance, like all the relationship postures, is another attempt to deal with anxiety. It can help lower intensities temporarily. But during the distance, one begins involuntarily to obsess about the one distanced from. The fantasies about the other are more intense than reality could possibly be. In this way distance creates its own anxiety, adding to the overall family emotional intensity.

A single father, thinking back about his experience in his nuclear family, described his efforts to think theory through some distant relationships. "I was in a sense a single father during the entire marriage (25 years). The basic emotional process revolved around my wife and two daughters. I was kept out. The more I tried to get in, the more I was pushed out by my wife. Since the divorce, there has been an ongoing effort to open the relationship with each child. The effort with the oldest continues to be productive. The youngest keeps distance, maintains superficial contact, and is immersed in her marriage and children."

Selden Illick, a psychotherapist and teacher of family theory, explains the difference between emotional distancing and emotional separateness: "Emotional distancing describes a pattern that individuals use to deal with the anxiety present in the relationship. Emotional separateness describes people's ability to move apart or together without acting out of any anxiety that might be triggered by the change." She sees the two being as on different ends of a spectrum. On the distancing end there would be higher levels of anxiety, more undifferentiation, more reactivity, and less thoughtful behaviors. On the emotional separateness end of the spectrum one finds lower levels of anxiety, more differentiation, less reactivity, and more thoughtful behaviors.

Distancing would be a relationship posture, whereas separateness would be a characteristic of selves with better boundaries. In separateness people stay in better contact.

Emotional Cutoff

The extreme of distance is cutoff. It is another of the three relationship postures where symptoms (mental/emotional or social) most frequently occur. In the sixties there was an epidemic of children cutting off from parents and running away from home. They were scared and did desperate acts such as taking drugs. They tried to change the world by joining movements, some with a theme of love, others angrily going to war with society itself—in universities, in the courts, or in the streets.

At the present time, cut-off, desperate kids may try to establish a substitute family by joining a gang. Also at war with society, they don't think twice about killing innocent people to prove themselves or make a point. This is an automatic, thoughtless attempt to solve a personal problem. These kids, like those of the sixties, though they might not see it, are trying to deal with missing family relationships. When the loss involves total cutoff, the intensity goes up to the point that reliable thinking is gone. Mindless behavior ensues, powered by the profound fury of the group.

Cutoff, like all the other relationship patterns or postures is an attempt to deal with anxiety. It says "If only I can get you miserable people out of my life, then I'll be much happier." Immediately after people cut off, when the anxiety has been seemingly intolerable, they do indeed feel better—for awhile. But, the initial euphoria of cutoff is very deceptive.

After the initial high of the cutting off wears off, however, some sort of symptom sets in—often depression or other bad feelings. The symptom can take the form, as the kids on the streets seem to want the world to know, of acting out. Or it can take a thousand other forms.

A great problem lies in relating the symptom to cutoff. Most people never do, perhaps because of that initial rosy glow one experiences immediately after the cutoff. From that one gets the idea that cutoff produces only good feelings. Also, the greatest majority of helping professionals are unaware of the phenomenon of cutoff and, hence, are unable to guide people through cut off relationships and out of their symptoms.

Because cutoff reduces the number of individuals in one's family system, anxiety will have fewer paths to take. This shrinking of the system has the effect of intensifying anxiety within it—it has fewer places to go. In that way it becomes that much more intense for the individual and symptoms ensue. Another effect is that the cut-off person will often go on replicating the cutoff in one important relationship after another, ultimately ending up isolated.

Andrea Maloney-Schara, a therapist and family-systems researcher, sees the increased divorce rate stemming from smaller nuclear families that are far more cut off from the multigenerational past. Because cut off families are smaller, there are less places for anxiety to go. As well, they have an ensuing larger investment in their nuclear families. This increases the relationship pressure the families are under.

Overfunctioning/Underfunctioning Reciprocity

It is possible to be too much the parent. A parent may feel over-responsible for the child, directing his or her every move, controlling each decision, or micromanaging friendships. When this happens parents unwittingly encourage the development of an indecisive, passive, nonplayer in life. Parents who were themselves oldest children in their family can sometimes be prone to this posture. But the pattern is certainly not limited to them.

One mother had a daughter who relied on her too much and the mother feared her child was becoming too dependent. The daughter hardly made a move without asking her mother what to do and how to do it. The mother gave some thought to this pattern and came up with a plan. The next time her daughter came to her and asked her what to do about some situation, the mother listened and instead of telling her what to do, as she usually had, she replied "I'm not sure what you should do about that—let me think about it." The daughter went off. A few days later, having heard nothing more, the mom asked her daughter what happened with the problem she had brought up. Her daughter answered, "I figured out what to do myself."

Isn't that what we're working toward? When we don't pretend to know all the answers we encourage the development of resourcefulness and thoughtful problem-solving in our children. How will children grow into responsible adulthood except in a gradual step-wise fashion, taking more and more responsibility for their lives? If we are always there with the answers how will they ever learn to struggle through to their own?

In the opposite of overfunctioning, an underfunctioning parent may, in effect, treat a child as if he or she were the parent. As is sometimes seen when the parent is a youngest and the child an oldest, the

parent can inappropriately rely on a child. It is as if the parent refuses to grow up, forcing premature adulthood on the child.

One father (youngest brother of brothers) and his son (oldest brother of brothers) who worked together had a relationship where the son was in charge of the father's monumental temper. When things got intense the son would become dictatorial. This had the effect of cooling the father down so that everyone could get back to work. Unfortunately, by relying on his son for emotional control (a job he would better have taken on himself), this father was playing his part in encouraging his son to take an overbearing, know-it-all, even tyrannical posture in his important relationships.

Communications

Communications in each of the patterned postures are typical, and can be mistaken for the problem. Whenever people have a relationship problem they often see it as a communications problem, which definitely will be present, but when they see only the communications difficulty they are missing the underlying relationship disturbance— the repetitious posturing that is going on.

In the child focus, communications are anxious and worried. They are mostly about the child because the focus prevents having an effective, satisfying relationship *with* the child.

In conflicted relationships, communications are intense. Invectives are hurled and blame is assigned. Sentences begin with "You" and end with irresponsible, thoughtless accusations and condemnations. The combatants often dredge up problems of an earlier period in the relationship or repeat criticisms of a former generation.

In a distant relationship, communications founder, the child and parent having very little to say to each other at all.

And in an overfunctioning position the parent does most of the talking, mostly giving advice for the youngster, sounding preachy or teachy. In an underfunctioning situation the parent says too little and puts the child in the advice-giving mode.

Once a child develops a significant symptom, for more than a short time, however, we can suspect a child focus that is worried and anxiety ridden, whether or not it takes a conflictual, distant, or

over/underfunctioning form as a kind of overlay or alternating posture. *The communications give us clues about underlying patterns.*

All relationship patterns and postures are more evident and intense during times of societal regression. As the anxiety in society infects families, the relationship postures snap into place. Finally they grind into ruts, making it more difficult for the relationships to function cooperatively.

Parents can work toward an understanding of the family as an emotional unit and how relationship patterns and postures operate within it. Knowing about these emotionally based relationship patterns, and being aware of the pitfalls, parents can get the focus back on themselves, their own relationships and extended system. Becoming more thoughtful, and having more of a relationship base for themselves, they will be able to manage themselves better in relationships with the younger generation. As this happens, the offspring take on new life.

The Wonderful Range
of People and Families

P
eople differ in their ability to adapt to life. Over a lifetime, some do better, some less well. People can be placed on a theoretical scale that describes numerically the fact that people vary in overall adaptation to life. The spectrum that describes this range is called *the scale of differentiation of self.* The concept is similar in some ways to an older concept of emotional maturity in that they both describe life adjustment. Differentiation of self, however, goes further than the old concept. It delineates specifically how the difference in people is thought to come about (in a relationship system) and outlines much more precisely how people vary in functioning. Further, the newer concept includes not only emotional and social adaptation but also physical health and well-being in its measure of life functioning and course.

It is important to realize that differentiation of self may look different at different times in life and so could, if it were possible, only be measured accurately over an entire lifetime. For this reason it is difficult to imagine that a way to judge the level of differentiation more than very approximately will ever be devised.

Even though it cannot be pinned down exactly in testing, the concept of differentiation of self is a pivotal one to the Bowen family systems theory. As people try to improve their functioning in relationships, it becomes extremely useful to individuals.

The theoretical scale, describing how people adapt to life, ranges from 0 to 100, depending on several factors, all intimately related to each other:

- Amount of *basic self* present
- The tendency to *fuse* self into relationships—amount of pseudo-self or functional self present
- The tendency to *fuse* or confuse thinking and feelings
- Degree of anxiety and ability to deal with stress
- Degree of permeability of self boundaries

All these characteristics are related quantitatively to each other. They could all be measured simply by amount of basic self—or any one of the others, if we knew how to measure them.

Basic self, the part of an individual based on *principle* and absolutely *unnegotiable* in relationships, is thus the part that tends toward individuality—the *differentiated* part of us. It can be thought of as having an impermeable boundary around it. *This is where principles reside— those well thought-out beliefs that act as an internal guidance system for the person.*

Pseudo- or functional self, on the other hand, fuses into relationships and contains beliefs that are not absolutely intellectually clear. *In that part of self are unexamined ideas we have been taught, or feeling-based thinking.* It takes on or gives up self in relationships. This happens more when anxiety increases and at lower levels of differentiation. Thus it can be said to have a permeable boundary around it, since self is taken on or given up in pseudoself, through this theoretical boundary (see figure 12).

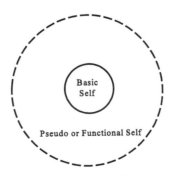

FIGURE 12

Theoretically, at zero on the scale there is no basic self and people function entirely out of pseudoself. At 100, people operate entirely out of basic self and have no functional, or pseudoself. No one is actually at either of these extremes. Rather, everyone falls somewhere in between these two points on a spectrum or scale. So everyone has some degree of pseudoself operating as well as some reciprocal degree of basic self. While intelligence is a gift and would tend to be an advantage in adaptation, some very intelligent people behave in an immature way in relationships. Also, people of high social standing may actually be low on the scale of differentiation.

Lower Levels of Differentiation

At the lower end people have more difficulty in life and there is more anxiety more of the time. As anxiety goes up, more trouble is triggered by unreliable or illogical thinking. That in turn results in inappropriate or inefficient decisions and behavior. As life problems mount, they elicit more anxiety, each in turn driving the other. Relationships tend to be overly dependent or stormy and cut off, taking up most of the life energy so that little else of value is accomplished. The relationship difficulty at lower levels on the scale has to do partly with the greater tendency to fuse self into relationships, a consequence of greater pseudoself (see figure 13).

Lower Scale   Mid Scale   High Scale

FIGURE 13: RELATIONSHIP FUSIONS

To the degree that selfs fuse or join emotionally with another, they lose some of their ability to act, think, and feel autonomously, an uncomfortable situation for both (or all three in the case of triangles).

Part of the relationship interference derives from the ambient anxiety carried at that range, making it hard to really connect. That anxiety drives unreliable thinking. Decisions are made anxiously or impulsively and so do not work out well long term, bringing on more difficulties. Principles are nonexistent or not well thought out, being based on what one has been taught on feelings. Core ideas and values have not been thought through to clarity so there is nothing solid upon which to base decisions or behavior. Much of the life energy at the lower end of the scale is taken up in relationship problems and focus.

Thinking and feelings are confused with each other at lower scale functioning so that what one thinks may be actually based on feeling rather than logic. Thinking is often described in feeling terms—that is, a feeling/thinking fusion also exists. For example, if you ask someone at this level what he/she thinks, the answer might be "I feel rather shaky about this whole thing." That is not a thought but a feeling. If asked what he/she feels, we might hear "I feel that this family is headed for a rocky time." That is not a feeling but a thought. These people do not really know the difference between feelings and thoughts and so there is very little choice in whether to operate out of the feeling, or the thinking part of the brain at any given time.

At the lower end of the spectrum, with its greater load of anxiety, there are more of life's problems in symptomatic form such as the various disorders—social (delinquency and addictions), mental/emotional (brain disorders), and physical (illnesses and accidents of many types). These symptoms, once they develop, increase the anxiety load, which adds to the tendency toward symptoms, and so on and on.

Higher Levels of Differentiation

By contrast, at the higher levels of differentiation, relationships are more cooperative, with less loss of self. People are less needy and dependent upon one another. They fuse self into relationships less, so more autonomy of selfs exists. Less fusion of self in relationships makes them work better. There is less anxiety. That also adds to relationship success as well as to success in life in general. When people have fewer relationship problems they have more energy to devote to the rest of their life goals. Life is guided by principles, which act as a guidance system for thinking and behavior. Decisions, better thought out and based on guiding principles and logic, have better outcomes, short and long term.

At higher levels people know the difference between thinking and feeling and their language reflects it. Asked what he or she thinks, one of these people might say "I think if all the facts are considered, including the pros and the cons, it is beginning to look more and more to me as if this family would benefit by making the move we are considering." Asked how he or she feels, an individual might say something like, "I feel anxious and a little angry at the moment but I am working on it—can we talk more about this in a day or two when I am a little more calm?" Though aware of their feelings they might not always choose to reveal all of them. Able to see the bigger picture more of the time, they are aware of more choices rather than feeling boxed in by the emotions or impulses of the moment. They can choose either thinking or feeling more easily. Faced with dilemmas they can, using their principles for guidance, think things through to a decision or course of action. There is more choice in how one feels, too.

People at the high end of the spectrum can develop symptoms (illnesses or accidents) but it takes greater levels of stress for them to do so. Given enough stress, individuals at any level can develop the most severe symptoms and illnesses. This phenomenon was first understood during the world wars. Not everyone developed battle fatigue, but everyone would, given enough battle exposure. "Every man has his breaking point," those wartime psychiatrists learned.

Life at Mid-Levels

Life at the mid-levels is somewhere between those two extremes—not as difficult as at the lower levels, because of less anxiety, fewer relationship difficulties, and fewer self-generated difficulties. But life is still not as easy for individuals at mid-levels on the scale of differentiation as at the higher levels.

Every point on the scale carries with it a slightly different quality of life than every other point. It may take a great deal of time and effort to move one's level of functioning up even one or two points. But even that amount of change will make for a very different life course (see figure 14, on the next page).

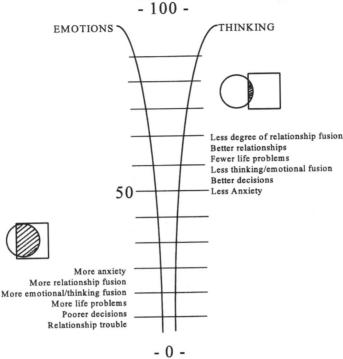

Scale of Differentiation
- 100 -

EMOTIONS   THINKING

Less degree of relationship fusion
Better relationships
Fewer life problems
Less thinking/emotional fusion
Better decisions
50   Less Anxiety

More anxiety
More relationship fusion
More emotional/thinking fusion
More life problems
Poorer decisions
Relationship trouble

- 0 -

FIGURE 14

This variation among individuals means that some people obviously are going to be better parents. No license or certification is required for the job. A calmer person who makes better decisions and functions freer of symptoms will do better at rearing the young.

Kathleen Kerr, teacher, writer, researcher, and clinician, observing the rhesus monkey populations of Stephen Suomi, at the National Institutes of Health, could see a real difference in mothering styles that varied from calm and appropriate to neglectful and also worried—over-concerned, over-watchful, nervous mothers. A perceptible spectrum definitely existed. Her findings in studying the data coming out of the chimpanzee studies of Jane Goodall at Gombe Stream, Tanzania, were similar.

It only takes a stroll through the supermarket to see that there are definite differences in the competence of parents.

High-Level Parents

To make those differences more explicit, let's look at some more characteristics of relationships in families where parents are higher on the scale of differentiation. They include separate boundaries, an equal posture, and openness in communications.

Separate boundaries means, for one thing, that when one person in the family is upset or anxious, the others are less susceptible to take on the anxiety. One can be with an upset family member without taking on the problem (or leaving). It also implies less intrusiveness. The intactness, or permeability, of boundaries makes it more or less possible for people to "give up self" in relationships (see figure 15).

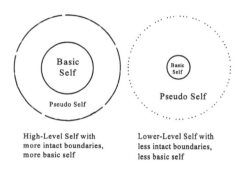

High-Level Self with
more intact boundaries,
more basic self

Lower-Level Self with
less intact boundaries,
less basic self

FIGURE 15

Parents with more intact boundaries know and state what they can and cannot put up with. They also respect and understand their children's boundaries. Boundaries are such an important hallmark of differentiation of self that the two characteristics to follow—equality and openness, really grow out of that feature.

Equality in the spousal/adult relationship postures makes it possible for the parents to share in the child-rearing and other "nesting" tasks in a complementary and team-like manner devoid of competitiveness or domination/subordination. This attitude of equality the adults have for each other engenders the same attitude toward the young, moving toward an equality stance with them as they move on toward adulthood. People relating from an equal relationship posture never have "respect" issues in their interactions with other people.

Openness means that people in higher functioning families usually are aware of what they think and can express that accurately and appropriately to others. They can wait to speak, when necessary, until they are sure of what they think. They are also open to hear what others think. Talking and listening are valued skills in these families. Individuals tend to listen about as much as they talk.

The regressive tendencies in present-day society affect everyone, even the families higher on the scale of differentiation. The facts of the regression may increase anxiety but higher functioning individuals and families are better equipped to deal with it. They are clear as to what their principles are, and are led by them instead of by every fad or wind of society that blows. Just as people vary in their ability to adapt, whole family groups do also, even in regressive times.

Examples of the differences in how parents deal with societal problems in the home are seen daily in every psychotherapy practice. If evidence pointing to a child's experimenting with illegal drugs is found in the home, a police attitude may be taken prematurely by one type of parent, focusing on the child and making a problem where none really existed. Drug testing, endless lectures, or therapy may be instituted immediately, though they are beside the point and unnecessary (though any or all of these may be appropriate at some times with some kids).

In another family, the parent defines self to the group clearly. "This is certainly nothing I would want anything to do with, but everyone has to live his or her own life according to his or her own principles," for example. Defining of self is not telling the other what to do, it is a statement about self—an "I position." The openness of the relationship system insures that everyone in it knows pretty much what everyone else thinks about most important topics.

The relationships between parents and kids in higher functioning families are such that there is no need for the young to rebel and take the opposing point of view except for the sake of argument (to think something all the way through in conversation, for example) and exploration—even high-level kids have to make their own mistakes. In this kind of relationship system the conduct of the young can safely be left up to them. This is a posture of obvious trust in the child's good decision-making ability. It is not misplaced when the parent's relationship with the child is friendly (open), trusting (moving toward equality), and respectful (observes boundaries). At the end of the day, *it is that relationship that wise parents know makes the biggest difference.*

Eileen Gottlieb, a Bowen theory consultant, believes the most important factor in being an effective parent is the knowledge of self. She says, "With a more objective understanding of my own life (what I think and believe, what I am up against) the more I have to offer my children. Yet, the clearest statement a parent can make to children is the life that is lived—a legacy we bequeath to our children."

As society spirals deeper into its regression, how do we build a life and a parental relationship built on the principle of differentiation of self? For one thing, it becomes more important than ever before to understand how young people, and for that matter, all of us, build an inner guidance system. For adults, the task becomes one of *continuous, thoughtful, inner dialogue.* Many people leave this, their thinking work, undone. But if that work is attended to, principles become always clearer and a working part of self. A guidance system made of principles begins to take form. These principles can always point the way in both important and everyday decisions and actions. It becomes possible, referring frequently to one's inner guidance system, to come out knowing, "This is where I stand" and why, on important issues.

The other equally hard work, that of being a self in our important relationship systems (home and work) involves awareness of boundaries. As boundaries become less permeable to the passage of anxiety between selfs, we become less reactive and intrusive to the others around us while maintaining good contact with them. Boundaries maintained in the family, with one's spouse or in other adult relationships and also with youngsters, result in a generation whose members are free to hear what we think, and are respected for what they think. That happens precisely because they are not so emotionally fused into family relationships. Boundaries make possible the open communications and equality that are so characteristic of these families (see figure 16 on the next page).

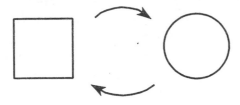

FIGURE 16

An ideal relationship is equal and open, with intact boundaries.

The families these young people form in turn are more differentiated to that degree (see figure 17).

Less fused into family relationships

More fused into family relationships

FIGURE 17

Parents, then, can concern themselves with understanding as much as possible about the generations of families that went before them, relating from principle to each other, their own families of origin and the younger generation. When an understanding of differentiation of self guides their efforts, it clarifies their own inner guidance belief system and directs their behavior to a level of parental competence they would not have guessed they possessed.

Bowen summarized the concept this way:

> "Parents can 'help' the child the most by each working on his or her own 'self.' This leaves the child freer to develop and grow in his own direction. On one simple operational level, this requires that parents work away from the parental 'we-ness' toward each becoming an autonomous self. Operationally, I have called this the 'responsible I' position. The parental 'we-ness' is made up of two separate people. The goal is to focus on the individuality and functional separateness of each, rather than the togetherness. Parental "we-ness" refers to one phase of the emotional undifferentiation between the parents, in which parents present themselves as a oneness in terms of beliefs, life principles, philosophies, and feelings. Each spouse came out of his or her own parental family with about equal levels of 'differentiation' from his or her own parents.

> "The lower the levels of differentiation the more they will strive for the perfect togetherness in their own marriage. And the more they achieve this togetherness, the more they encounter complications of this 'stuck-togetherness.' One partner, for instance, fuses into the self of the other and becomes a functional no-self, vulnerable in later years for some kind of physical or emotional illness or social irresponsibility, or one or more children become incorporated in the parental immaturity. In some instances, there is a mixture of the various combinations.

> "The 'responsible I' position by parents is a way of reducing the intensity of the 'we-ness' or the family "stuck-togetherness" and moving toward the healthier differentiation of selves. The responsible self assumes responsibility for his or her own life, happiness and comfort. He tells himself, 'I am going to be the most responsible self I am capable of becoming. I am going to live within my own life space, and be responsible for myself, and not tell the other how he is to live in his.'"

This is the opposite of selfishness. Bowen continued:

> "The more family members assume responsibility for self, the less self-centered and selfish each becomes. In any family there are two emotional forces. One is the powerful force of togetherness that operates as automatically as a reflex; the other is a calmer and more thoughtful force toward individuality, differentiation and self-determination.

"When one family member takes a step toward individuality or differentiation that is not dictated or approved by the family system, the togetherness side predictably attacks with accusations of selfishness, self-centeredness, not caring, not loving, and other similar comments. If the differentiating one can stay on course without counterattacking, or defending self, without rejecting, the family upset quickly subsides. Family members then express appreciation to the differentiating one, and then, later, others in the family will make similar moves toward differentiation. The 'responsible I' family member accepts responsibility for self without blaming others for his unhappiness or failures. The more immature family members overlook the 'responsibility' and misuse the 'I position' to gain selfish wishes, 'rights,' and 'privileges.'"

Why Children in the Same
Family Turn Out So Differently

W
e have seen how family anxiety, when it comes to rest in a
child, can have extremely untoward results for the child.
How is it that children in the same family can turn out so
differently? Some seem so emotionally mature and others, in the same
family, extremely immature or even symptomatic. To see how that
works, let us take a look at a typical family.

The P Family

When their first child, Alex, was born, Frank and Pat P had just taken
over the management of Frank's father's family business. There had
been some disagreement in the extended family about the succession,
but Frank had finally been chosen CEO, and Pat managed the office.
Shortly after that, Frank's father and Pat's mother died within days of
each other. The P family was typically a rather high functioning family but with four nodal events occurring so close together, the anxiety
level was extremely high.

The baby was colicky, and some thought the high level of family
anxiety had something to do with it. At any rate the colic focused
most of the family anxiety on the boy. After that there were many infections, pneumonia, and bronchitis with repeated visits to the emergency room and hospitalizations. This went on for several years.

A sister was born when Alex was five. By that time the effects of the
grandparents' deaths were less pronounced on the family. There was

less focus on the daughter and, predictably, she had fewer problems. By the time the third child, a boy, was born, the extended family business issues had been resolved to everyone's satisfaction and the business was doing well. He also received less focus and also had few problems.

The P's, anxiously focused as they were on their first son, by worrying about him as much as they did, in effect dumped most of their anxiety onto him. This insured problems for him. In his case, they were physical. They might as easily have been mental/emotional or social. No one knows what process determines the difference in symptoms. In any event, his level of differentiation was different than that of his siblings who, progressively a little freer of the family self-fusions and emotional process, came out a little higher on the scale. For life, the three would all be operating at different levels of inner and ongoing anxiety and thus they would all have different abilities to cope in the world (see figure 18).

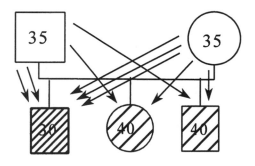

FIGURE 18

This tendency for parents to focus more on one child and less on another, with resulting differences in the levels of differentiation of their children is the *family projection process.*

This concept, along with the fact that families have to deal with different amounts of anxiety at different times in their life histories, accounts for why we see one child with very poor functioning and another with high achievement, both in the same family. If the greatest

load of family anxiety happens to center on a child during the first six years (formative of personality and perhaps of differentiation), life will be different for him or her than for other children in the family whose years before six were calmer. As we have seen, if the child develops symptoms as a result of the focus, typically the symptoms will only serve to draw more focus through the years. The other children in the family will be a little freer of the family emotional process. Each child in a family has a very different experience of that family and, in a sense, each has a completely different family.

How children come to be the focus of family anxiety is an interesting study in itself. As we saw in the P family, overwhelming stress can have outcomes in a family that would not be predicted. Had not so many stressful events occurred together in the life of the P family, their relationship with their first child could be presumed to have been quite different.

Other families can "choose" a child for other reasons—though this is, of course, not a conscious, thought-out process, it is automatic. A focus might get going because the focused child was in the same position as someone who did not do well or had a severe problem in the parent's family of origin. Another might receive the projection because he is the first, or the youngest, or had a birth defect or other problem at birth. Anything that makes a child a little different can, it seems, draw parental anxiety. There are almost as many "draws" for the projection process as there are families!

The fact is that projection of family anxiety rarely if ever occurs evenly or to all the children in a family. Rather, it tends to focus on one more than the other—to siblings in different amounts. So children in the same family do turn out quite differently from the standpoint of differentiation of self. If the family projection process were fair, it wouldn't focus on children at all, it would resolve the anxieties in different ways, depending on where it belonged and in more effective and appropriate ways. But neither life nor families are fair and sometimes their usually adequate and effective coping strategies get overwhelmed. Sometimes families are totally unaware of how they are "doing in" some of their members or how they might be able to handle anxiety differently had they a different way of thinking about relationships and anxiety.

Because the regression is still developing and deepening in society, and as it touches all of us, families will, of course, experience increasing amounts of anxiety. Children born later into the societal regression will, all things being equal, tend to be born into more anxious families and other societal groups—one more factor unequally affecting each child's experience.

Parents working from family systems principles do not try to relate to each child the same. Each child, for many, many reasons, including genetically, is different. They will, however, know that an anxious focus on children is detrimental to their optimal development and life course. So, insofar as possible, they try to contain their own anxiety, processing it within the self, with each other, and the extended family system, rather than developing anxious, focused relationships with their children.

How Anxiety Travels Through Generations

Anxiety travels in a major way between two generations, as described by the ideas of child focus and the family projection process.

Since this phenomenon is always going on and on throughout time, we can sometimes, if we look, see the inexorable march of anxiety throughout the generations in a *multigenerational emotional process*.

Victoria Harrison, family systems researcher, consultant, and teacher, describes it like this: "Most people think about multigenerational transmission in terms of genetic or behavioral influences, both of which assume that the individual or interaction between individuals are the unit of transmission. Bowen theory sees the phenomenon in a different way. The family over the generations is an emotional system. Individuals are connected to each other over several generations and influenced by how each generation manages in the face of challenges presented by life and by each other. Levels of differentiation of self determine differences in how one generation affects another—the constraints, the flexibility, the strengths and symptoms—how they are all passed along."

People have studied many different topics encoded into their extended family generations, such as reproduction, ideas about death and dying, money, dominance of women, dominance of men, addictions, and many others. All these long-term and ongoing studies not only enrich the understanding of the researcher about his or her own family heritage (and thus of self) but also extend the details of family theory in some important ways.

Just as different siblings from the same family can wind up with quite different levels of differentiation of self, the branches of an extended family that these different individuals establish can trend upward or downward in their functioning. In that way, certain branches of the same extended family evidence a greater number of problems than others.

Parents interested in increasing their own level of functioning in their families and in life try to understand as well as possible the generations of their own families. This search for understanding has taken many people on some interesting journeys. They have included reestablishing contact with cut off branches of their families, searches in records in this country and abroad, and trips to cemeteries, nursing homes, and old family homes.

Learning about the generations of our own families shows us how family anxieties have come down to us in the present. When we are tempted to give way to feeling states of over-responsible guilt or inadequacy, we can remember that *we are only part of a very large, long process*. All this has come down to us and is in us. Although it may seem at times that our children got a bad break in their parents, really we are only the latest in a long chain of handling the stresses of life in certain ways. We may be able to do our part a little better with principles. But we are only a small part of something much larger. The multigenerational look describes what is, and has the possibility of removing blame as people try to do the best they can in relationships with their children.

One family researcher had always been plagued with a fear of abandonment she had never been able to understand. She studied her family back ten generations. As she did so she realized that in each generation on her mother's side there had been at least one very early death. This study was important in her effort to, "feel better." The sense of connectedness she gained meant that the fear of abandonment was gone, except in intense crisis situations.

Eileen Gottlieb is studying survivors of the German holocaust. She is finding that viable family relationships—the ability of family members to be a resource to one another—make a difference in life performances of the survivors. She sees that families who know their past, attain some degree of objectivity about it, and remain connected to each other, do better in life than those who do not. She sees being a parent as intimately connected with a multigenerational emotional process emanating from an interdependent relationship network. Understanding how perceptions are passed down through family lines, affecting one's own life is important in rearing children because the more one understands about this process the freer one can be of it.

Gottlieb sees functioning as the outcome of multigenerational patterns of management of acute and chronic anxiety and the position of each person in the relationship system. Depending upon one's degree of knowledge and objectivity about this process, as well as the existence of and participation in family relationships, people are more or less vulnerable to developing symptoms.

People often express the impossibility of putting into words the enormity of what this search for family connections and information has done for them. The grounding aspect of the experience is often referred to. However people describe it, there is no doubt that it is a positive and helpful adventure. For many it is neverending.

Many parents have an intensely curious and appreciative audience when they communicate what they have learned about the preceding generations of their family to their kids. This seems to be another way to make sure that cutoff does not become patterned in the family. Parents who are not cut off from former generations of their family do better at making opportunities for the younger and older generations to be together and develop relationships. In doing this they live out one of the basics of family life, showing what family is all about—the emotional connectedness and groundedness that can only come from the group we were born into.

Birth Order, Personality, and Relationships

Walter Toman showed, through research with thousands of people, that not only are we influenced by our place among our siblings but also that the place our parents occupy among their siblings has an indelible impression upon us. Bowen incorporated Toman's research into his theory as the concept of sibling position.

The B Family

Sibling positions of parents and offspring affect their personalities, their interactions with each other, and the kind of relationships they tend to form. For example, Sarah and Paul B, early on in their marriage, formed a relationship posture of overfunctioning/underfunctioning reciprocity. Sarah, an oldest sister of brothers in her family of origin tended toward leadership around Paul, a youngest brother of sisters. She had more of the ideas and energy. He was content to follow her lead much of the time. Sarah was surprised and chagrined as she increasingly discovered that their son Bob did not appreciate her ideas and initiative, and butted up against her as often as he cooperated with her. He was an oldest, too, and as such had many of the same leadership qualities of his mother.

His dad would follow along with him much of the time, as would, of course, his younger sister, Patty, born two years after he was. She and her father both had that youngest's sense of humor that could break up the whole group into laughter whenever the two oldests got a little intense in their disagreements. Both of the children were also influenced in their personalities by the different qualities of their same-sex parent. So Bob could at times follow, if necessary, and could even crack a joke at times. Patty knew from her mother how to take the lead if she had to though she found herself following along more often.

There are almost countless combinations for nuclear families to create according to sibling position alone, since there are eleven of them. They are—oldest brother of brothers, youngest brother of brothers, oldest brother of sisters, youngest brother of sisters, oldest sister of sisters, youngest sister of sisters, oldest sister of brothers, youngest sister of brothers, only son, only daughter, and twins. Middle children have some unique characteristics also—they tend, often, to be peacemakers and may have great relationship skills. They usually display one of the above positions too, since they are usually connected more strongly to one of their siblings than another, so they will be like an older or younger to someone else. The strongest connections usually occur in siblings closest in age.

The point, as in all of family theory, is not that we are stuck with what we are born into. Rather, that is where we start. Toman does not believe that birth order accounts for the major part of personality. But to the extent that it does define where we are, we can use this information for understanding ourselves, our family members, and their/our relationships. With this knowledge we are in a position to plan how we will work our way out of the limiting aspects of our position. *The higher families and individuals are on the scale of differentiation, the less birth order determines and limits personality.*

In the case of Sarah B, her realization of the influence of birth order on the scratchy relationship between herself and her son opened a door. She could see that if she continued to dominate the relationship with him, he would end up denying important strengths in himself. In this relationship she was bringing out many of his as well as her own negative attributes. By putting the focus there, she was making sure they would permanently imprint on his personality. She backed off from conflict with him, finding other options for her own conduct when he would become bossy or overbearing. She tried to be more calm around him, to not always have to have the last word, and to encourage his leadership traits instead of be threatened by them.

At the same time, she attended to her relationship with her husband. She suddenly saw how she anxiously lorded over him much of the time, preventing him from being much of a self around her and then complaining about it. This didn't feel good to either partner and yet neither had a way to think about making a shift. Predictably, as Sarah worked on her relationship functioning with these two and also with her siblings in her family of origin, her relationship with her daughter improved also. She could see everyone in the family flourishing as she kept the focus on herself, always trying to "do herself" a little better. In this way, Sarah's understanding of the concept of sibling position introduced her to a way of working on improving her version of herself in all her family relationships.

The increasing anxiety in society, families, and individuals, may have the effect of making it harder to see options, promoting a "stuck" feeling. It may feel as though, having been born into a particular sibling position there is little one can do about it. But theoretical principles indicate that *creating superior personal choices and improving one's life functioning are always possible, even in a regressed, anxious environment.* Thinking systems, working toward differentiation of self, and focusing on the bigger picture it fosters can point the way toward being freer of what we were born into.

Parents who are aware of the concept of sibling position can see how the particular sibling position of each person in the family has positives or strengths associated with it. They can focus on and applaud those strengths in everyone, rather than focus on the weaknesses. This creates the opportunity for people growing up in the family to maximize their talents and abilities. The awareness of birth order will also tend to help them to avoid certain attitudinal traps in their relationships with their children, such as overprotecting the first child, giving the oldest too much responsibility too young, or babying the youngest.

By knowing the weaknesses of each birth position, parents can encourage movement out of those tendencies. For example, they can expect a youngest to assume a fair share of responsibility. They can provide an oldest with opportunities for playing and being a kid.

As children see the grown-ups working on being more grown up, they will predictably work on their own immaturities. This is not something we can do for others, even if they are the children we brought into the world.

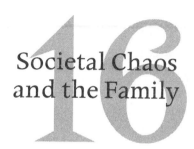

Societal Chaos
and the Family

We have noted that an extremely important concept for us today is that of societal regression. It means that society goes through times of increased anxiety and disorganization that lead to poorer individual and family functioning. Irresponsible, childish, illegal, rebellious, even outrageous and outlandish actions become commonplace. *The behavior of only the few is consistently guided by principle rather than anxiety, either in families or in the institutions of society.* Society's institutions, set up and depended upon for insuring orderly living, sink to the regressed level of the day. It becomes difficult if not impossible for them (human services, courts, police) to process their workload. The ordinary citizen seeking assistance from these service agencies cannot get through to them, finds they are bogged down with overload, or that they seem to have little or no interest in doing their jobs.

These conditions prevailed for many years in the Soviet Union before its demise. With the attempt to institute democracy, things have only become worse, democracy depending, as it does, on a responsible citizenship. It would appear that many other societies in the world have been involved in regression that goes back a very long time.

What triggers the regression? After the downward spiral begins it is difficult to tell how it was triggered in the first place or what keeps it alive. John Calhoun studied overpopulation leading to crowding in mice and rats. He found that under these conditions anxiety in individuals skyrocketed and normal societal roles between and among individuals broke down. Is overpopulation responsible for societal regression? Or, does overpopulation lead to lack or degradation of resources? Franz deWaal points out that two of the densest populations among humans are highly organized and not regressive—the Netherlands and Japan. Is it because of fear of nuclear, chemical, or bacteriological annihilation of the species?

Another postulated trigger for societal regression is the economic downturns that seem to inexplicably occur from time to time. Also, we have referred to the fact that psychological theories influence parents and society at large.

This is not to say that regressive theories aren't in some sense born out of regressive times and thinking—the social climates no doubt play a role in producing theories. But once created and publicized they can, at the very least, greatly add to the problem. Joseph Campbell, the great scholar of myths of different cultures, gave close attention to this very point. In studying the myths of different cultures, he came to the conclusion that artists and other mythmakers (leaders) profoundly influence their societies, not the other way around; he did not believe myths were merely a product of their times.

The Role of Therapy in Shaping the Regression

Some of the foremost mythmakers of our day may be the "therapy professions." In some way these professions and the principles for living they put forward may have been, unwittingly and incredibly, important factors leading to the societal regression. While psychotherapy may have helped large numbers of people in some ways, there may be other ways that they put individuals and society itself on a downward spiral. The therapy disciplines (psychiatry, psychology, social work, and some ministers) at present seem to be dominated by a way of thinking and a procedural method that often adds to the problems in a family. Perhaps they have added to the problems of a whole culture, since so many people seemed to adopt, wholesale, the principles of these professions as their personal guidelines for living. Specifically, some of the beliefs and teachings that may have worked in this manner would be: focus on the individual instead of the family, focus on pathology (what is wrong) instead of strengths of the individual and family, a feeling-orientation at the expense of rational thought, the pleasure principle, and permissiveness in rearing children.

Without a way to see the family as an emotional unit, there is no way of approaching family relationships for better functioning. Without the big picture of families, the focus narrows to the individual and on his or her "pathology"—what is wrong with and in every person. Unfortunately, the more people focus on their weaknesses, the less they seem able to deal with them and the weaker they become.

In addition to the focus on the individual and his or her pathology the helping professions became preoccupied with feelings as the way to address the pathology. Any and all feelings were encouraged in the psychotherapeutic setting. As they uncovered feeling after feeling, these intense sessions only served to find still more emotions to explore. When the "feeling catharsis" was encouraged as helpful to relationships, many marriages caved in under the intensity.

A major technique that tried to address children's problems—play therapy—was invented to address the problems of disturbed children. Just as adults talked out all their feelings, children were encouraged to bring out all feelings and emotions in play. Any and all behavior was accepted and valued. Therapists "stood in" for parents instead of coaching them.

Through popular books, guides for parents, and accounts of social experiments where children were given free reign, parents of several generations were introduced to ideas originally intended for use in the therapy situation in psychoanalysis. They became guiding principles for parents. The idea of allowing as much behavior as possible for fear that undue restriction—with attendant "repression"—might bring about negative effects in their children meant that parents tried to become as "permissive" as possible. In many families it became difficult to determine if anyone was in charge. Things were often out of control, and children seemed to rule the roost.

A principle of helping professionals akin to permissiveness is the pleasure principle—perhaps reactive against mores and values that seemed to many to be restrictive of the human's optimal development. What started out as seeking pleasure in life—long term as well as short term—became for many, instant gratification as a way of life. Long-held values regarding sexuality, the family itself, and parents as leaders in the family were questioned and discarded. If a marriage didn't feel good any longer, terminate it. If an affair felt good, go for the pleasure.

Pollster Daniel Yankelovich notes that "our society now places less value than before on social conformity, respectability, and observing the rules, on correctness and restraint in matters of physical pleasure and sexuality. Higher value is now placed on things like self-expression." One cannot help but see a connection between the changing ways our society thinks and behaves and the values espoused by a great majority in the therapy professions.

It is possible that many factors—theories, environmental pressures, economic downturns, and any other source of anxiety that can be named—all somehow work together to produce the mass chaos—regression—we live with today.

One thing is certain—whatever the cause, when society is in regression all its members are more anxious than they would be otherwise. Living in an anxious, regressed society constitutes an enormous stress for families. It becomes more difficult for them to function as well as they do in less regressive times. Just as individuals have their breaking point, so do families. Given enough stress, not only individuals, but also the groups of which society is made—families being the most basic and important—can develop symptoms.

At the same time, anxious families strain society by producing individuals with problems and then expecting society to address the difficulties. The families themselves are often at a loss to know how to assist its own members to higher functioning. So there is a mutual process whereby families and society each influence the other in the downward spiral. In this sense we must all take responsibility for regressed society's direction.

John Calhoun, in research at the National Institutes of Health, found that as a population of mice was allowed to become too dense, anxiety increased and the orderly mouse "society" declined into regression. As it became disordered certain predictable instinctive parental behaviors were lost. One of the skills lost was the ability of the mother mice to build orderly, characteristic nests. At the same time, the male mice, who under normal circumstances would parade in wide circles around the perimeters of the nests in a kind of guarding behavior were nowhere to be found.

Given enough anxiety, families and other important societal groups split apart with increasing frequency. Not only do we see a large number of divorcing marriages but also large numbers of businesses and government organizations dissolving or recombining into new forms. And of course, all of this affects families.

The Effects of Anxiety

Let us remember again the effects of anxiety. Anxiety circles and reverberates in a family system. Depending on the level of differentiation of the family, it passes more or less easily from member to member in the group.

In the body, anxiety sets off a chain of physical events affecting many if not all systems. It is preparing the organism to meet an emergency situation—the blood pressure goes up, as does the heart rate, providing more nutrition and oxygen to muscles and the brain for quick action and decision-making. Antibody production is reduced, blood clotting facilitated, and digestion put on hold for a calmer time. In an emergency, these physical changes are absolutely necessary for survival.

If the anxiety continues, either triggered by a series of emergencies or perceived threats, or if the ambient anxiety is high enough over long enough time, either generated inside the family or outside it, as with societal regression, these intricate and interrelated physical systems can trigger illnesses from a lack of antibodies against foreign substances or from poor digestion, for example. Physical symptoms will, of course, elevate the anxiety even more.

In the brain, the capacity for logical, reliable thinking is diminished if the anxiety is strong enough and persists over a long enough period of time. Endocrine and neuroendocrine systems become exhausted. When this happens, people, including parents, make poorer decisions. Ongoing—chronic—anxiety interferes with their relationships so that as the level of anxiety goes up, relationship patterns and postures tend to snap into place. If these postures become stuck in ruts, they generate additional anxiety of their own, as do physical symptoms. A vicious cycle begins and perpetuates itself.

Continued anxiety also seems to put individuals and groups on auto-

matic, so that they do more of what they have been doing, and do it more intensely. It is harder for them to create novel solutions, or ways out of the problem. Emotionally based relationship postures and patterns intensify and increase, and parents act at a lower level of differentiation than they are capable of in other circumstances.

A Baby Boomer Family

Susan and Ron G grew up in reasonably well put together families. But they were children of the '60s. They, for different but similar reasons, found their families oppressive and adopted generally rebellious attitudes. They went in and out of the drug scene together. Their marriage relationship could best be described as a cocoon in the early years. They met in San Francisco, to which they had run from their families, and it was the two of them against the rest of the world. Their relationship was strengthened by various causes with which they aligned themselves, but they stayed extremely cut off from their original families. When Susan became pregnant they went off drugs and were married. Sometime after that, the cocoon relationship became more one of conflict and distance. When things were most intense, one or the other would use marijuana. This would create more distance as well as intensifying the conflict.

The drug use was, they thought, well hidden from their children. But it should have come as no surprise that their focused child's problem was that of dealing drugs in school. (There are of course, many families in this society who have no history of even experimenting with substances, including alcohol, whose kids are getting involved in that problem.)

When family relationship anxiety, whatever the trigger, is not resolved, as we have seen, it can come to reside in any member of the family. But all too often it is a child. For that reason, if research looks only at the "identified patient," which most does, it understands only part of the story, since it does not see the entire emotional unit.

The G's child's drug dealing got their attention. They took a long hard look at themselves and the family system they had created. Their marriage, born in cutoff, was missing an important resource— their extended families. Inevitably, the pattern of conflict and cutoff had been replicated over and over in their life together. They began an effort to make some basic change by establishing contact with their families. Their parents and siblings were surprised but warm and welcoming. As they improved their relationships with their parents their marriage became more direct and cooperative. Their drug use disappeared.

They were glad for this but realized they had an extremely distant relationship with their problem child. Each parent tried to establish contact with him. The court system, which they were forced to negotiate, though difficult and symptom-focused itself, actually reinforced their efforts to make contact with their son. Either they worked together as a better-functioning family or the results would be dire.

Their child's pattern had been to divide and conquer. He would go to each separately for permission, getting different answers, get them involved in an argument over him and slip out unnoticed. As their relationship improved, he tried to do this even more, seeming to want to draw the focus. However, the two parents found a way to cooperate in their own relationship to the extent that they no longer could be divided into conflict by their son. After a few tries, he got the message that there was something different in the family. They each separately were also getting more of a relationship with him. In time, he dropped his devious practices in favor of the better level of functioning his parents were now evidencing. There was no longer any need for rebellion.

In times of societal regression, the nuclear family unit is threatened not only by the increase of anxiety everyone in the world is experiencing, but also by regressing norms of behavior. What, at a different time would have been labeled unacceptable behavior and not tolerated, is now often seen as par for the course and not unusual. Families do not know what to do nor how to take responsibility for the behavior of their members. Drugs or weapons at school elicit less and less alarm as their prevalence increases. Teens are educated about sex. It is accepted as inevitable and considered a subject for school involvement. Condoms are distributed. Abstinence either in drinking or sexual activity is held out as an option only rarely. Our children have to deal with tempting choices that would have been unthinkable in other generations.

The regression threatens all institutions of society, including the family itself. It has elevated divorce to such a live option that there is little or no incentive for adult children of cutoff to work on spousal relationships. Without relationship guidelines it seems infinitely easier to them just to leave and start over again than to make existing relationships work better. Little do people realize that if the level of differentiation is not changed they will only reestablish the same level of problem—though perhaps not in the exact form—all over again in another relationship, perhaps another family.

Parents taking the high road, using differentiation of self as a guide for decisions, communications, and behavior in general, can stay present in the family they have created, thinking their way through to a better level of relationship functioning—a principled way of behaving in specific situations. They can use family systems theory and whatever other guidelines and beliefs they value and cherish to become a higher functioning individual and family. They can, where cut off, reestablish relationships with their families of origin and also find ways to be present and accounted for in those groups. They can make opportunities for the younger and older generations to connect with each other.

A high-functioning family can be an island of logic, clear thinking, and connectedness for each other in a chaotic world while not cutting off from it. They may even find ways to connect, from principle, with the regressive forces themselves. They will find ways to say what they think and believe in. When enough people begin to do that, the regression will be on its way out.

Where most people are seeking quick fixes, simple answers, and easy methods, few want to take the trouble to think at all, let alone to think theory.

A few will. Those few are an extremely important group, and they may be all it takes to make an enormous difference in society. Those few can change trends.

Sometimes it only takes one. Roberta Holt, Bowen family systems consultant and teacher, looked at what it takes in order to calm the anxiety in society. In researching the Salem witch hunts, she found that the leadership of one person actually brought them to a close. A member of the famous Mather family did this by making a statement that he believed the witch hunts should stop. This he said, calmly and dispassionately, to various conflicting segments and factions in the community who were at odds with each other. As he did this the societal brouhaha gradually calmed down and disappeared.

Part Three

Parents
Connecting

Present and Accounted For

There is an old story of a traveling father. He always brought his young son a gift when returning home from each of his many trips. Once he came home without a present. As his son searched his pockets, his dad explained, "The gift is me myself— I'm home, and I just want to be here more with you."

Almost all parents would say they love their kids (whatever they mean by that), wanting the best for them, having affectionate feelings for them, taking pleasure in their achievements. We certainly develop some kind of bond by simply spending time together, as we do in families. All this and more may go into the definition of love. Perhaps we each need to write one. But love, however one defines it, is not enough. Neither is being responsible, caring, being attached, giving, prioritizing, sacrificing, or even staying home when one would rather work. Many families with all these qualities are now producing children with problems on a regular basis.

Well, then, what is it that children need from us? What are our goals as parents?

Many people have told therapists through the years what it is they really needed and wanted from their parents. If we can think about what relationship system we are daily helping to create, our offspring will benefit and be grateful. Therapists can attest to the fact that people don't blame parents for the regressive state of society. They don't mind so much whether their parents made a lot of money or not. They can even understand two careers. But they do remember and thank their parents, or not, for the legacy of relationships in their family. The relationship legacy the younger generation would optimally receive from us as parents would include at least five parts:

1. A cooperative marriage relationship between parents where each functions as a self. Failing an intact marriage, a well-functioning adult friendship system and the ex-spouses, continuing to do their relationship work, can make the difference for the single parent.

2. A relationship with parents that is calm, thoughtful, attentive, and based on principles.

3. Smooth-running relationships between each other as brothers and sisters.

4. Relationships with the extended family members of each parent that are there not only for holidays and reunions but also throughout life, sharing joys, understanding pain, and standing in when and wherever necessary.

5. A concern and feeling of responsibility for the wider community, using its resources judiciously and helping it to work better by an attitude of responsibility and giving back to it.

Therapist Fran Ackerman thinks there are four aspects to being a parent:
1. Nurturance
2. Allowing appropriate independence
3. Limit-setting
4. Value transmission

In the first two of these she sees the parent/child relationship laying down the individuality/togetherness balance the child will carry on through life. The second two are where parents define self in the relationship with their children.

How do successful parents think? What do they do? How do they do it? Many books, articles, and periodicals have been published in an attempt to answer these questions. There are several magazines devoted entirely to the subject of parenting. Most of these are "quick fix" or technique-oriented, "how-to" advice prescriptions. The problem with how-to's and fixes is that they apply only in a given situation.

Unfortunately, life has a way of always coming up with something different that is not covered by the technique.

Sometimes parents go around asking all their family and friends what they would do in a given situation. Then they take a vote, and that is how they make a decision.

Some have traditional, individual-based theory in their heads. These people tend to get more and more into how everyone is feeling and less and less into how to actually solve or resolve anything, even the feelings themselves. Rather, they are engaged in a project of forever whipping up more and more feelings in self and in others. They forget that talking about feelings, even in therapy, may have limited value. Taking this approach in one's relationships probably has a destructive effect on the very relationships one is attempting to address. Talking about feelings may seem to help in the therapy situation because of the well-known cathartic effect of ventilating. This approach is less effective in real life, because the anxiety usually merely moves over to someone else in one's system, adding to the circulating chronic anxiety in the system.

If, instead, parents have in their heads a theory that points out a better way of handling themselves in the family relationships, rather than a how-to that will apply in only a limited number of situations, or promote a constant wallowing in feelings, they have guidelines that shed light on every possible circumstance, including their thinking, feeling, and behaving. They will find that gradually they go on to a better level of functioning in the family and that in time, the family joins them up there at that higher level.

Faced with a dilemma, it can be helpful to think through the concepts of theory to see which ones apply. This exercise is useful to calm the frustration within self, because thinking calms the emotional brain. By approaching a dilemma with principle-guided logic, solutions emerge.

Bowen family systems theory is a set of principles, not techniques, that many families have found invaluable as they struggle and grapple with the enormous problems coming at them from within as well as from society in regression.

The Most Important Goal for Parents

Giving kids what they most want and need from us—a relationship legacy—may be best achieved if we also have another goal for ourselves as parents. This goal kids could never put into words—it is personal to each parent—but will support the previously mentioned relationship goals perfectly. It is the goal of *raising one's level of differentiation of self.*

Working on going to the next higher level of differentiation of self will be a project unique to each parent, because, depending on where each is on the scale, the next-higher level on the scale will look/feel/be different for everyone. What it would take to get to that next higher level will vary, depending on where people are starting. Thinking through to clarity on this goal may take some time. The specifics of the goal will change as new information is gained, as thinking is done over time and as people actually change in the direction of meeting their goals. This work is for self—a parent's mission. It may be best written out and referred to from time to time.

Though differentiation of self is not entered into for the sake of anyone else, as basic self grows, there will be an effect on one's nuclear and even extended families.

One effect of parents raising their level of differentiation of self is that they will then produce a generation with as high a level of basic self (differentiation) as possible. One can picture selfs in the family becoming less and less in emotional fusions over time and in better and better communication.

As parents differentiate more self from the family group, children are, by definition, freed of fusions (immaturity, undifferentiation) they would have otherwise carried on into their own adult relationships. Many children, freed of worried focus have displayed a blossoming that might well be described as a bird's being let out of a cage.

How the steps to take, and efforts to make, would look in a specific family can be listed and/or drawn in pictures. This will be the most exciting and rewarding of all possible projects, and the one out of which other creative projects and opportunities will flow in an amazing succession.

The Goal of Parents is Not

- To get your kids to be or do what you want them to
- To become what your kids want you to become
- To get your kids to think the way you want them to think
- To think the way they want you to think
- To think, feel, or behave the way your family of origin or your spouse's family wants you to think, feel, or behave
- To think, feel, or behave the way your spouse wants you to think, feel, or behave
- To think what your minister or the wisest person in the world thinks
- To be liked

No one can do this thinking for you. It is your task alone. *Thinking is hard work.* But no one ever accomplished anything without goals, so continually formatting what differentiation would look like for you is one of the most rewarding tasks you can ever carry out. It is a first step in raising one's level of functioning and in creating the relationship legacy we would all like for the next generation.

By now it is obvious that we cannot build self in anyone except ourselves. If, however, we are true to this task, and in emotional contact with those in our families, the children will automatically leave home with more basic self than if we had not turned the focus and effort toward improving our own functioning in life.

If we tell the people growing up in our families what to do or how to think, we are increasing fusion of selfs, not increasing self boundaries in them, nor in ourselves. As well, if we anxiously focus on them, we increase the fusion and decrease basic self. The same can be said of all the other relationship postures—conflict, distance, and cutoff. They all are evidence of and at the same time further promote fusion of selfs.

The more regressive forces of society will tend to diminish and derogate, perhaps even fight against anything or anyone that looks like the presence of basic self (differentiation). Having principles or taking a stand may, during regressed times, appeal only to the few. It will also appeal to whatever differentiation of self is present in the others, but a warning is in order: Brick bats are usually thrown at those who decide to take that high path.

Parents working on differentiation, however, when they are sure about an issue, do not hesitate to hold calmly to their principles. Nor do they keep quiet when it is the appropriate time to define them to others. If thought is given to how others can best hear an "I statement"—"This is what I think or where I stand"—these messages will be heard better. Differentiation also involves taking appropriate action for self at times. Others may protest the action. But when parents stay on course with their thinking, their communications, and their actions, the protest dies out in time and the family goes on to a higher level of functioning.

18

The Emotional Nucleus
—the Parents' Relationship

The *nucleus of the nuclear family is the emotional relationship between the founding adults of the family—the parents.* It is their level of differentiation that sets the general limits for the family. The apple does not fall too far from the tree. It is also their undifferentiation and relationship problems that set the tone for the emotional interaction problems in the whole unit. So *if there is one most important gift we can give to the next generation it is that of a solid and satisfying marriage relationship.* Out of that partnership flow and unfold the triangles, temperaments, and relationship propensities of another generation.

Notions such as sibling rivalry and adolescent rebellion have been made, by traditional theory, to seem normative for the family. However, seen through the lens of differentiation of self, they both may be more a reflection of unresolved parental issues than necessary phenomena in all families. Some families seem to take out their undifferentiation in addictions. Others show their undifferentiation in physical symptoms, and yet others in mental or emotional problems or conflicts with the law. Kids' undifferentiation does not necessarily play out the same as that of their parents, however. They may be so "allergic" to their parents type of problem that they avoid it like the plague and then proceed to go to the opposite extreme in their effort to be different.

Understanding and working on self in the emotional systems we were born into and those we create does not in any way negate all the scholarly work that is being done on genetic factors. It does, however, demonstrate the tremendous influence of the family emotional system. Perhaps genes themselves may be influenced by the family emotional process in some way that is not understood at present. It may be that many factors are needed to work together to produce a symptom. Certainly the emotional system factors, while not easy to grasp, are to some degree understandable, and more so as one works with them. And, while they are not easily manipulable, they are there in self and in the system to work with for basic change.

Although the needs of children are often insistent and sometimes emergent, the parents' marriage is the emotional basis out of which the adults' relationship needs are fulfilled. So it must be given whatever focus it needs to keep it running smoothly. It sets the emotional tone for the family. Anxieties here must be resolved within individuals or among spouses (or adult relationships) themselves or they can eventually show up as a symptom in the young. Keeping anxieties where they belong will prevent their spilling over into other people.

Phil Lorio, a psychiatrist who uses Bowen theory in his practice, believes that because the family is an emotional unit, it is impossible to be an effective parent while being a poor spouse. Likewise, one needs to have a good relationship with oneself in order to be an effective spouse. This is impossible if one is emotionally cut off from one's parents, siblings, and family of origin. So he sees the real challenge as being true to one's own individuality, to constantly develop self while simultaneously respecting and promoting the individual development of the other. Being the best individual one can be in the context of one's larger family relationship network is the primary indicator of our effectiveness in every relationship.

Dr. Lorio believes in the *overriding importance of principles, beliefs, and convictions strongly held and consistently practiced in our everyday lives.* To him, effective parental leadership is achieved by an ongoing personal development process in which one is always striving to become the most solid self possible. It is never completed, but rather is always ongoing.

Another psychiatrist, Jerry Lewis, studied 50 relatively problem-free families to see what made them work so well. One of the major factors he found was that the parents were interested in their own relationship and took time on a regular basis to be together without the kids. Their children loved knowing the parents had a special relationship that did not include the kids. It felt right to everyone.

It is often said that parents must present a united front. Unless one person is being done in in the relationship, however, this almost never happens. If the spouses are working toward an open, separate, and equal relationship with each other they will have a cooperative kind of leadership in their family and know how to work things out.

Murray Bowen explained:

> "Before starting family research I accepted and practiced the united front of the parents as one of the soundest psychological principles. The reasoning was that the united front prevents the child from playing off one parent against the other. Family research and family psychotherapy have led to the conviction that it is one of the most unsound principles.
>
> First, there were the observations in very disturbed research families in which parents could never agree on the right way to treat the child. Finally, in a sort of exasperation, when family turmoil would be high, one parent would take a stand, such as, "I don't care what anyone else thinks or does. This is what I believe, and what I stand for, and what I am going to do." These would be clear, definite, and non-angry statements, which I later came to call the "I Position." As soon as this parent had taken some action based on this statement, the family would become amazingly calm. Then, when the other parent would also begin to state "self" more clearly, the issues about the united front would disappear, and the whole family would make a dramatic move toward health.
>
> In 15 years of family psychotherapy I have not seen a contradiction to the thesis that the united front is an unhealthy situation. It is healthy when each parent can have a separate and different individual relationship with the child. The united front presents the child with an amorphous parental amalgam that is neither masculine nor feminine. A child with a separate relationship with each parent is in a better position to know men from relating to his father, and to know women from relating to his mother. There are other important aspects. The united front is not a constant thing. It is invoked when one parent is anxious and unsure. The effort to arrive at a united front is primarily to relieve parental anxiety and not for the benefit of the child. I believe parents have been using this through the centuries, in anxious situations.

Dr. Bowen explains that parents playing off one or the other against the child or the child playing one parent off against the other is all part of the functioning of any triangular emotional system. It is a

two on one situation designed to force the third to accept the opinion and decision of the other two. When successful, it relieves the tension between the parents, and calms the total triangle temporarily. It results, however, in a more difficult long-term situation for the child. The child, dependent upon the parents, has fewer options in counter moves to deal with the parents. If he accepts the parental edict, he is impinged. If this impingement continues repeatedly, he is impaired to some degree. A more energetic child will fight back, even if he has to use desperate moves.

Fortunately most united fronts are spurious in that one parent pretends agreement that does not really exist. The child, being aware of this, can then use it to some advantage in his counter move. However the outcome, the united front presents the child with a locked in 'two-on-one' situation that is difficult for him to adjust to. This is one of the ways parental immaturity is transmitted to children. A child who consistently 'gives in' will emerge as an adult who is 'done in' by life's later 'two-on-one' situations. The child who fights back will later become a master at playing off people against each other. Almost all parents will use the united front principle periodically when anxiety is high, while the most insecure parents use it consistently and forcefully.

Therapist Katharine Baker thinks it unnecessary for a couple to agree about approaches to child rearing, but creating a calm, respectful, and engaged environment in the family will teach children a great deal about becoming a responsible adult.

Therapist Fran Ackerman does not think parents need to present a united front. She calls it a myth among some parents and family therapists who confuse a united front with not undermining one another. Parents can—and usually do—have different points of view regarding what children can and cannot do. Parents do need to clarify issues between each other so that the child cannot work one parent against the other in the family triangles. Defining of self becomes the key idea in this kind of a process.

If the united front is not an option for high functioning families, then how best can we think about parental leadership in that "emotional nucleus" position? While parents will not agree on everything involving children, they will at best have a solid enough relationship with each other that when disagreements arise they can resolve them with each other. The kids do, after all, need an answer to questions about what they can and cannot do at certain ages. A couple operating as a cooperative team will find ways to give the kids what they need from them, including boundaries as well as many other decisions and actions without undermining and contradicting each other. Neither partner needs to lose self in a cooperative relationship even though neither wins every decision. But one or the other may, at times, have to make a conscious decision to follow the lead of the other if it is the more logical thing to do. Conscious decisions to support one another do not involve loss of self. Knee-jerk reactive postures and patterns do.

Societal regression tends to make divorce seem an easy option to dealing with problems. When books and counselors are advocating it and all one's friends are doing it, how does one keep the family unit on course if the going gets really rough? Theory can help. It shows that if you don't solve your relationship problems with one spouse it is unlikely that you will with another. The reason for that is that one attracts people at one's own level of differentiation, which means that the tendency after divorce is for people to simply recreate the same old problems within another family. *So the only sure way out of relationship difficulties is to work to raise one's level of differentiation of self.* Your spouse will, in the vast majority of cases, rise to meet you at your increasingly higher levels. Then the relationsh will work better. If you are divorced already, you will meet and attract a higher level person in your future relationships.

Societal regression presents unprecedented problems for parents. It encourages feeling-based behavior and thinking rather than clearheadedness. It presents opportunities for destruction and self-destruction unknown to former generations. The accompanying mounting anxiety makes it harder for all relationships, thus tending to split apart all society's groups and/or cause them to malfunction, including, especially, the family. But principles can help people stay grounded and on course, individually and as a family group.

Parents guided by principle, however, have a relationship apart from that with their children. They take time for their own relationship—quiet time, fun time, whatever time they need to make their relationship into what they would like it to be. They do not approach each other from feelings alone, although they are important and necessary if they are going to endure as a unit. But also, when the going gets rough, these parents can call relationship principles and clear logic into play.

Connecting with Our Children

After the parental relationship, which sets the emotional tone and provides leadership for the family, the relationship we have with our kids is next in importance and will have a great deal to do with how the rest of life goes for them.

During consultations with parents about their troubled kids, one of the first questions is, "Do you have a relationship with this child?" Next, there is usually a pained poignant silence. Predictably, more than 90 percent of them admit upon thinking about it that they really have very little meaningful, functional connection with their troubled child. They may worry about him or her a lot but really do not have a person-to-person connection—a relationship. If there are principles concerning this, the first one must surely be—*be sure you have a personal relationship connection with each child in your family.*

Let's consider that relationship. If the ideal relationship is separate, equal, and open, perhaps those ideas can help to describe the process of connecting with another generation. So let's look more closely at each of the qualities of a high-level relationship, the kind we'd all like to have with our kids.

Separate Boundaries

When parents really get the idea of separate boundaries—a cornerstone of openness and equality—it seems to unlock a great deal. Is it really possible to remain calm and thoughtful when your child is anxious, ill, or in trouble? Maybe only to a degree, but to that degree, boundaries are being observed and parental functioning is calmer and more thoughtful.

Ms. B

A single mom, Ms. B was a relative newcomer to family theory. She got a call from the police in the wee hours of a Saturday night concerning her 16-year-old son. "We have Sam in custody and would like you to come down and pick him up."

"What has happened?" she asked.

"He was found in possession of an alcoholic beverage. Ma'am, if you don't come down here and get your kid we're going to have to take him to juvenile detention overnight."

"May I speak with him?" she asked.

Sam got on the line. "Mom, will you get right down here and pick me up right away? If you don't they're going to take me to juvenile detention."

"I am afraid to come to that part of town by myself at this hour but I'll see if your father will come," she said.

A call to Sam's father was made. He declined to go.

More calls came from the police rudely ordering her to get down there.

At this point Ms. B tried to "think theory." She realized that her son had gotten himself into a bit of trouble. If she went there without allowing the natural consequences to have some effect, his problem would become hers. If the problem stayed with him, they would both learn more, she reasoned. (There had been a time when she would have rushed down to rescue him without thinking twice.)

Her answer to the police and to her son, by turns, was that she was unable to come at this time but would pick him up in the morning. Both the police and her son were unhappy with her, but a pickup time and place were arranged for the following morning.

It was a matter of boundaries. His problems were his, hers were hers, and there was a difference. Now her dilemma was—how to get to sleep. She knew if she could sleep the rest of that night she would be functioning in family relationships at a higher level than ever before. So she relaxed and went to sleep, her relationship boundaries getting a little more shored up, and operating a bit better after that.

Twenty Ways to Invade Your Child's Boundaries

For most of us, invasion of boundaries is all too easy. A very few examples would be:

1. Tell her what to do when you know she knows what to do

2. Dress her when you know she can dress herself

3. Check his room needlessly

4. Take too much part in school activities

5. Talk about him to his brothers/sisters

6. Talk about her to her friends

7. Worry

8. Hover

9. Make a bigger deal than necessary out of hairstyles and dress codes

10. Think about her more than you do yourself or your relationship with your spouse

11. Ask too many questions

12. Have too many rules

13. Always have to win at games

14. Overschedule him

15. Don't allow any alone time

16. Demand certain friends; prohibit certain others

17. Treat her as if she were younger than she really is

18. Let his achievements determine your sense of emotional well-being

19. Take on her unacceptable behavior as your own problem without letting the natural consequences do their necessary work

20. Make him or her eat everything on the plate

Twenty Ways to Allow A Child to Invade Your Boundaries

1. Answer all questions

2. Ignore kicking or screaming or other unacceptable behavior that is affecting other people

3. Need to always be liked by your kids

4. Need to always rescue

5. Allow children's "divide and conquer" technique to cause trouble in your marriage

6. Feel you must buy/supply anything asked for whether you can afford it or not

7. Defer to children on making major family decisions

8. Don't lock your bedroom door when you want time alone

9. Worry about your kids when you are out for the evening

10. Lose sleep because of unresolved curfew behavior

11. Allow your children to decide what you think about things

12. Allow your child to sleep in your bed past infancy

13. Be unable to articulate to your kid what it is you really think about important issues

14. Be unable to have fun on a vacation or never go on one without the kids

15. Allow your children to take your things without permission

16. Drop everything on demand

17. Allow a child to interfere with your marriage

18. Allow your child's tantrums to keep you home when you need to go out

19. Never say no to community child-oriented activities you really don't want to do and/or don't have time for

20. Make your kids the center of your life

These boundary violations may be obvious to some. It would be easy to think of twenty more. But one could take any of them to the opposite extremes and be in as much trouble. Never answering any questions, not ever allowing kicking, even appropriately, never rescuing, and so on and on—would only be the opposite side of the coin. What would that say about boundaries—would they be any better? Of course not. Extremes in relationships always mean a relationship problem, which always means a boundary problem. In a distant relationship one might try to argue that there are adequate boundaries. But actually, distance is just another form of fusion and blurring of boundaries. Were the boundaries better there would be no need for distancing.

Toward Equality

Out of those better boundaries we are always working toward comes an increasingly equal relationship stance. Although equality may not seem appropriate in a parent/child relationship where parents are properly in charge, one of the goals for parents surely is, as the child grows into an adult, to attain a relationship of equals with their offspring. Ideally, this is built gradually, from day one. There is a way of relating that acknowledges the child's equal worth as a human but still makes clear the authority of the parents in the family. Some parents have a surprisingly equal stance toward even their toddlers. Others never reach equality even though their children are quite grown up chronologically.

When one constantly tells a child what to do, or gives answers, instead of encouraging his or her struggle to find their own way whenever possible, the self of the child is denied in the relationship. A relationship of an "oldest" parent with his or her youngest child may fall into such a pattern.

Sometimes parents look to their children for direction. In this case, the child is denied parents and a childhood. These kids will not get an early look at parental leadership that will enhance their own ability to be in charge in a nuclear unit later on. Parents in the "youngest" original family position are sometimes prone to relating to their oldest child from a more dependent stance, especially if they are in anxious circumstances.

When the parents/adults do not have an equal relationship themselves, of course, it is of primary importance for them to work toward a better posture with each other. If the offspring are denied the gift of seeing how that operates close up in their parents, it makes their own relationship tasks with peers that much more difficult.

Open Communications

Openness, like equality, more or less flows from separateness of selfs. When people know and work to preserve their emotional separateness, they know others do not know what they are thinking/feeling/about to do, so they want to let them know. They talk (define themselves). They are just as aware of their need to know what is in the mind of the others. They listen. In this way their connectedness is one of two separate selfs.

Many parents today are quite afraid to say what they think. They have been devalued and blamed by the helping professions to the extent that they often feel safer keeping quiet. In addition, most parents in consultation have believed their kids do not care or want to hear what they think. The effect of all this is to stifle any effective communication from parents.

The biggest contributors to the communications breakdowns between parents and kids are the anxious relationship postures that lead to ineffective communications. If parents are always telling offspring what to do or think (overfunctioning/underfunctioning reciprocity), the kids will often tune them out. If they are always critical (conflictual), the kids will fight back or tune out—again no meaningful communication takes place. Tiring of all these ineffectual attempts at communication, parents and kids alike will eventually stop saying anything to each other at all (distance).

Parents Defining Self

Parents are usually shocked, shaking their heads, when told "Your kids really do want to know what you think."

"Right," they say, "that's why he tunes out every time I start to talk."

Nonetheless, it's true—they do want to know what we think. But when we tell them what to think, fight with them, or don't say anything at all, we are not simply telling them what we think. We have taken a relationship posture that will not work. And defining self, telling them what and how we think—the guiding principles of our own lives—is the only thing that other people, kids or adults, can really hear. It is the only kind of open communication that is not born out of an anxious relationship posture. Defining self clearly, thoughtfully, and effectively is beautiful to hear and it can be heard by others.

Also, whether we realize it or not, kids do hear a tremendous amount of what parents say. Think about it—what can you still hear your parents saying in your head to this day? Just as Lorenz's goslings were imprinted to him (they would follow him or the first object they saw after hatching), our kids are imprinted, in a similar way, to us. Our children learn to speak a language that we speak in the accent and terms we speak it in. They may walk like us. Our interests and ideas shape theirs.

Unfortunately, many of our communications tell our offspring messages we, upon reflection, would not want them to get. Anxious parents sometimes, in an effort to get their kids to "shape up," resort to ridicule, sarcasm, put-downs, or name-calling. They do not mean most of this. But, until kids are quite advanced in their ability to think, they are unable to unscramble the real message behind the literal words. They take them at face value. These emotionally triggered, negative messages make a lasting impression in the emotional part of the brain and stay there, often becoming a part of what people think about themselves for the rest of their lives, a part of their guidance systems. It is important, therefore, for us to be extremely selective in our choice of words when anxious, especially if we are saying anything at all to our kids pertaining to them.

The largest study of adolescents ever done, sponsored by National Institutes of Health, found the *connectedness children have with parents* to be the most powerful factor determining whether they use drugs and alcohol, attempt suicide, engage in violence, or become sexually active at an early age. It was far and away more important than any other factors the researchers could identify.

The study recommended that parents take certain steps—set high academic expectations for children; be as accessible as possible; send clear messages to avoid alcohol, drugs, and sex. They also recommended locking up alcohol and getting rid of guns in the house.

Because parents are the leaders of the family their effect on their children is profound. For this reason Bowen family systems consultants involve themselves mostly with the parents in a family. Parents working on differentiation of self will see fewer and fewer problems in their children as their own functioning and their relationships with their children improve.

Phil Lorio, a psychiatrist and a father, believes effective parents have as a lifetime goal to be the most solid, grounded individuals they can. He means by groundedness, in part, having clear principles and strongly held convictions and living up to them whenever possible. One example of a principle would be the importance of personal responsibility for self and for all of one's behavior as well as responsibility to others. Responsibility to children requires taking care to avoid being overly helpful to a degree that one impairs their functioning. He admits it is a tightrope act and one may err on one side or the other, but maintaining awareness and a calm observational posture will move one along in distinguishing the reality of the needs of the child as distinct from what one's own anxiety about the child would dictate.

Dr. Lorio believes that responsibility to a child also means developing good listening skills. He has found it helpful to spend some quiet time alone with each member of the family, working at being a calm, interested listener and carefully avoiding overtalking or lecturing. "Responsibility to a child requires the maintenance of discipline so that there are rules, and these rules are enforced: it is in this way that children learn to lead an orderly and principled life. Discipline should be enforced in a manner that communicates seriousness, but avoids excessive anger. A goal to head for is a posture of kind firmness. Without self discipline, a parent will not be able to effectively discipline children."

Ann Landers reports that Rev. C. Galea was assigned to the Guelph Correctional Centre for a summer. He asked the young lawbreakers to draw up a code for parents, and here is what they said:

Keep cool. Don't fly off the handle. Keep the lid on when things go wrong. Kids need to see how much better things turn out when people keep their tempers under control.

Don't get strung out from too much booze or too many pills. When we see our parents reaching for those crutches we get the idea that nobody goes out there alone and that it's perfectly OK to reach for a bottle or a capsule when things get heavy. Remember, children are great imitators. We lose respect for parents who tell us to behave one way while they behave another.

Bug us a little. Be strict. Show us who is boss. We need to know we've got some strong supports under us. When you cave in we get scared.

Don't blow your class. Stay on that pedestal. Don't try to dress, dance, or talk like your kids. You embarrass us, and you look ridiculous.

Light a candle. Show us the way. Tell us God is not dead, or sleeping, or on vacation. We need to believe in something bigger and stronger than ourselves.

Scare us. If you catch us lying, stealing, or being cruel, get rough. Let us know why what we did was wrong. Impress on us the importance of not repeating such behavior.

When we need punishment, dish it out. But let us know you still love us, even though we have let you down. It will make us think twice before we make that same move again.

Call our bluff. Make it clear you mean what you say. Don't compromise. And don't be intimidated by our threats to drop out of school or leave home. Stand up to us, and we'll respect you. Kids don't want everything they ask for.

Be honest. Tell us the truth no matter what. And be straight-arrow about everything. We can take it. Lukewarm answers make us uneasy. We can smell uncertainty a mile away.

Praise us when we deserve it. If you give us kids a few compliments once in a while we will be able to accept criticism a lot easier. The bottom line is, we want you to tell it like it is.

In a regressed society parents and kids find it harder and harder to get that all-important one-on-one relationship that both theory and next-step research say is the only real safeguard against the most troubling youthful sidetracks. Parents and their children have little time to spend with each other. Some scarcely have dinner together these days. Increasing anxiety means that anxious relationship postures will snap into place and often become ingrained. In the most extreme and intense families and times kids and parents will cut off en masse. When that happens the young are set adrift prematurely—with the even more intense anxiety of cutoff—to find their way as best they can. For some, this will mean a group of peers adopted as a substitute family.

Parents who understand the importance of having better connections with their children do at least three things:

1. They keep on trying to get a better connection. They work on doing their end of every relationship, including the ones with their children, always a little more calmly, thoughtfully, and on track, a little more dictated by principle. Believe it or not, kids want better connected relationships with us too, and in time, they will respond if boundaries are observed.

2. They prioritize the family and their roles as parents, and realize that relationships take time. They make time for relationships with their children, and find ways to spend time with them that they both enjoy.

3. They do not hesitate to define self to the next generation when needed and appropriate. They don't let the helping professions, or their kids, shut them up. They know their life experience is of value and that kids really do want to know what they think—that is, what their guidance system, on principle, says about various subjects and how parents call it into play.

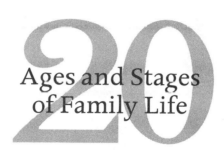

Ages and Stages
of Family Life

Parents, in producing another generation and guiding it through all the stages of development on the way to adulthood, accept several challenges to their own functioning and flexibility.

As children grow they go through several predictable stages of development that make varying demands on parents, from infants, who really need someone to be there all the time and even put them first very often, to teenagers, who usually need a great deal of freedom and who may need to hear "No" at times. As babies grow into school-age children and then into adolescents some parents will be able to be there appropriately. Some will not be flexible enough to make the shifts necessary, and so we see some parents treating pre-teens like toddlers or teenagers like preteens. So, at the very least, parenthood provides a wonderful opportunity to work on increasing one's own flexibility and adaptability.

Much has been written describing the expected behaviors and developmental norms for the ages and stages of development. These descriptions are important for parents, especially first-time ones—they take some of the mystery out of watching and guiding as a young person goes through the many changes on the way to being an adult. Of course, if one's child does not develop exactly "according to the book" these references can add to family anxiety. Einstein, and many others, however, were late bloomers.

Now we'll take a look at the consecutive ages and stages in which parents participate, from a family systems perspective. Of primary importance at any developmental period is the level of differentiation of the family—how it is functioning emotionally.

Conception and Pregnancy

Do relationships and reactivity have anything to do with the ability to conceive? In her research, Victoria Harrison, a practicing therapist, has examined these questions. Specifically, she has studied how family relationships impact the reactivity that governs reproduction. The biology of reproduction is influenced by relationships within the family, between man and woman, with parents, siblings, and the family over the generations. She sees that the hormones, biochemistry, and the nervous system are all affected by relationships.

One study she carried out was concerned with patterns of ovulation and family emotional process. "The women who did not ovulate experienced higher levels of stress all of the time. They and their mothers had contact with only a few members of their family. The relationship between mother and daughter was particularly intense, each feeling very responsible for the other. Most of the women who were ovulating experienced delayed ovulation consistent with intermittent stress and with contact with a large number of family members. Relationships within the family both stabilize and bring on stress reactions. Women who cannot stop having children they cannot care for are also living in a particular kind of family system that affects their biology and behavior.

"In consultation people can develop knowledge of their family and their biology in order to understand difficulties they face around reproduction and rearing a family. Women have conceived when they discover how to deal better with the pressures in the family, but reactivity within the family can override efforts to reproduce. Reproduction can threaten either the mother, the marriage, or other generations. If it does, symptoms develop somewhere. Levels of differentiation of self across generations in the family are key to understanding relationships, reactivity, and reproduction."

Anxiety and the Developing Fetus

Is it possible to think about the effects of anxiety chemically and/or anatomically upon the nervous and other systems of the developing fetus? There is evidence to suggest that babies from anxious mothers' pregnancies do not do as well as those from non-anxious mothers.

While the experiments to date have not involved humans it is likely that the same processes take place in the human, perhaps with even greater sensitivity. Myron Hofer reports "Nearly everything that experimenters did to pregnant mother rats and mice affected the behavior of their offspring." Various types of stressors including electric shocks, crowding, handling, restraints, or bright lights produced major behavioral differences from normal, even though the babies were fostered by normal mothers from birth. Especially affected were emotional and sexual behavior.

The offspring of mothers crowded during pregnancy took two to three times as long to emerge into and explore unfamiliar territory as agemates with nonstressed mothers. Male rats of mothers stressed by periodic restraint and bright light did not display normal male sexual behavior in the presence of receptive females and assumed female sexual positions when approached by normal experienced males. They were not only demasculinized but were also feminized as a result of their mothers' experience during pregnancy.

How can such an outcome be mediated biologically? Hofer believes that maternal hormones are changed in amount and pattern during stress, and act on the fetal brain and on endocrine glands to modify the neuroendocrine networks being laid down. These altered networks result, later in life, in altered behavior patterns. Other possible pathways from the mother affecting the unborn individual include stimulation of the various senses of the fetus, the mother's diet, her intake of foreign substances such as alcohol, tranquilizers, and opiates, as well as the control of placental function by the mother's uterine arteries.

Babies

With the birth of each child, the family goes through a nodal event—the addition of a person—a major event in the history of the group.

These can be experienced differently by different families and differently by the same family at different times. The impact of a birth on the group can range all the way from one of a fundamental threat to its existence to a fairly smooth assimilation of the new member. A new person in the group means new triangles are formed in the nuclear family, requiring major adjustments on the part of all—the structure and functioning of that unit becomes different. Thus, there are more pathways for anxiety to take and they are more complex. Functioning positions in the group automatically change.

It may not be possible to give each child an equal start in life since the facts of functioning of each family are different and also because each family is different, as we have seen, with the birth of each child. The family constellation is different for each child. Pressures and stresses are different for the family and in society at different times. Parental "takes" on each child—attitudes and fantasies—are different for each one. Each child comes into the world with a different temperament, eliciting different parental and sibling reactions.

Is it possible to think, from the very start, of a new life as a separate person with a separate identity and life course? Probably it is to different degrees in different families at different times. Some mothers relate more to their newborns as separate persons emotionally. Others see each baby more as an extension of self, and react intensely to every reaction of the baby. How much difference does it make, from the beginning, to be in a relationship with that baby that is perceived by the parent as eventually becoming one of equals?

How much does the nodal even of birth threaten the marriage relationship? The answer will vary according to where families fall on the scale of differentiation, as well as how connected families are with other generations.

Toddlers—the Explorers

The parent's challenge changes with the onset of talking and the child's mobility. Babies, so dependent on adult attention and nurturing for survival, while fulfilling and gratifying, can be draining for new parents. Even though toddlers no longer have to be carried around, they still require almost constant attention. They are out to see what life is all about, how everything works, and what is going on in the world. But they retract periodically, as if on a rubber band, to their caretakers for reassurance—some more, some less. In relationships, some toddlers are outgoing and friendly, wanting to share everything, and others are more quiet and to themselves This may be a function of sibling constellation—as well as how interactional patterns play out in a given family. This change from infant needs to the toddler's expanding world is drastic. Some parents can make the shift and respond appropriately to the toddler's energetic emergence of a self. Some have more difficulty.

Paul MacLean believes, from his study of comparative neuroanatomy, that audio-vocal ability developed in mammals in the "paleomammalian" brain in order to maintain contact between mothers and their exploring young.

Kathleen Kerr, observing the rhesus macaque monkey population of Stephen Suomi at the National Institutes of Health, saw great differences in youngsters. When faced with a newcomer observer, some displayed unabashed curiosity, while others cowered in fear at the prospect of an unfamiliar person.

As toddlers develop speech, they become assertive and exciting— even more interesting people. They know what they want and can tell us. They will "imprint" our speech—language, vocabulary, and accent. According to Deborah Tannen, communications researcher, their speaking styles will differ somewhat between males and females. Are these innate communication style differences or do these differences depend on relationship differences that boys and girls learn early?

Will we at this stage carry on interactive conversations with our toddlers, recognizing their personhood? Or do we see them as too different or too much a part of self to really relate to?

So the relationship problem for parents remains—to see the child as someone separate from self, reserving some of the focus for self, as in every relationship. This self-focus is not "selfish" or negative. Rather, it is necessary for parents at every stage of family life to be able to look at self and see what one is doing in relationships, how one is doing it, and where adjustments need to be made. And, it is of primary importance for that self-focus to respond thoughtfully in adult relationships in order for them to be alive and well-functioning. For some parents to see the toddler as a separate, yet valuable and interesting self will require a great deal of thinking and planning. For others it is automatic.

How does a parent preserve the child's safety and security and yet encourage socialization and creativity, as well as respect the increasing individuality that is beginning to emerge? All these constitute a huge responsibility for the parent of a toddler. But recognizing what are the important questions often seems to point one toward solutions. John Rosemond notes that

> Instead of sending children outdoors to play, we let them sit in front of the TV set for thousands of hours during their formative years of ages two to six. It is known that TV-watching interferes significantly with the development of a long attention span. Consider the fact that the picture on a TV screen changes about every three to four seconds. Because of this constant flicker, the TV-watching child isn't attending to any one thing for longer than a few seconds. As a result, the more time a child spends watching TV, the shorter his attention span becomes. Passive T-watching also competes with the development of initiative, social skills, fine and gross motor skills, and hand-eye coordination.

> Since 1955, when American children began watching significant amounts of TV, learning disabilities have become nearly epidemic in our schools. Interestingly, the symptoms that characterize a population of learning-disabled children and the list of developmental deficiencies inherent to the television-watching experience are one and the same."

Emerging from an optimal toddler stage, a child will have a fair command of the language. He or she will be running, playing, and even creating with artistic and other materials. Relationally, he or she will have experienced his or her family as non-anxious, friendly, caring, and helpful. Out of those early relationship experiences a trusting and cooperative attitude toward people will develop. A child will be able to tolerate some absence from the family. Many will have participated in early education programs. Many will have had several caretakers other than parents.

Along with the serious responsibility we feel for our young children, it will all, no doubt, go better if we can remember what sociologists have often pointed out—that primitive peoples know well what babies and toddlers are for—they are for having fun!

School-Aged Children—the Achievers

With kindergarten and school comes yet another shift for parents. Now children have some basic understanding of the world, competence in language, and ability to be apart from family for fairly extended periods of time. Now they need to master that world. In order to do that, the school-age years provide, optimally, continued and extensive opportunity to acquire an acquaintance with the culture and further physical and mental skills and abilities. Relationship patterns, laid down in those early years in the family are now exercised in a wider arena. The more differentiated kids (those with a higher level of basic self) will attract higher level people as friends. They will deal with all levels of teacher experiences more adequately, and in general, all things being equal (though every family has its breaking point) go through this broadening and learning time with fewer problems.

Much has been researched and written about encouraging and developing competence and self-confidence in children and helping them achieve. Research has shown that parental praise tends to encourage specific behaviors and disapproval or punishment tends to extinguish unwanted behaviors. This school of thought, behaviorism, using "operant conditioning"—rewards and punishment or aversive conditioning—has met with a certain amount of success in meeting some of the problems of kids.

Also, with "problem" kids, it has been shown that parental commands (in contrast to requests) for appropriate behavior can turn around some situations.

One can't help but wonder, however, after watching the effects of parents simply improving their relationships with each other and their offspring, if these methods work at least partly because of relationship improvements parents make in the course of implementing these techniques. The most powerful behavior modifying factor in a child's life is the relationship he or she has with his or her parents.

At any rate, during the school years, parents have an extended period to be with their children in many interesting ways. As kids' mental and physical competence flourishes, parents have opportunities to enrich their kids' and their own lives by being with them and taking part in activities and projects, as catalysts, coaches, and companions.

In these years, children's abilities to think and decide develop along with physical development. The beginning of guiding principles can be seen if you watch for them. Principles cannot be taught or given. One can be exposed to them but for them to end up as a part of basic self they have to be thought through and put into practice. As appropriate decisions are left to children, and as parents do not hesitate to define self to their kids, increasingly, they will learn responsibility guided by principle.

A worried focus, as we have seen, defeats the normal development of children—they will, if worried about, believe they are incompetent (or no one would be worrying about them) and act accordingly.

Parents Eliciting the Best in Their Middle School Children

Optimally, children will emerge from middle school years with skills in the three R's and the fourth—relationships (this one acquired at home, not at school)—that mean they are competent physically and mentally and have enough basic self to become the kind of teenagers that their parents were or would like to have been.

Parents can help their middle-school-aged children to be the best they can be by:

- Processing their worries in ways that do not focus on the kids— that is, by focusing on their own functioning and relationship with each other
- Being there in a day-to-day relationship of two interactive selfs that has separate boundaries, is open, and is moving toward equality
- Watching kids develop with interest
- Having fun and doing things with them
- Defining self—what parents believe and how they think
- Setting limits when necessary, enforced with thoughtful discipline
- Preserving time and focus for self and their marital (or adult) relationship system
- Providing as much contact with extended family as possible
- Allowing kids to choose and manage self in their friendships without parental micro-managing
- Encouraging responsible and thoughtful decision-making

- Catalyzing, rather than demanding achievement
- Enjoying their own lives

These ideas are only a few examples. Each parent, on reflection, creates their own ways to be the best he or she can be in each individual situation.

Teenagers—Launching Time

Now our kids are really leaping—physical growth is often astounding, and behavior can be too. Amazed parents may wonder, "Who is this person we have brought into the world?" This young person now has a history in the family and community, a definite personality, and a functional place in the family. The child may seem quite uneven in functioning, by turns, trying out being an adult alternating with leaps back to babyhood. For some, it is as if they are back on the rubber band again. Their rubber band snaps back and forth from adultlike behavior and thinking to the emotional tantrums or emotional roller coasters of the small child. This phenomenon will be more or less pronounced, of course, depending on the individual level of differentiation.

Anxiety in the family unit stems from several sources. First, everyone senses the importance of this beginning time of separation from the unit and wants to complete this phase well. Certain crucial life tasks will be grappled with now. Ethical and behavioral principles are worked on and taken as a part of the character—for example, standards regarding right and wrong, sexual behavior, drinking, drugs, and social behavior. During this period also, dating may begin. A vocation may be chosen.

Anxiety in the family with teenagers is also escalated if the adolescent experiences inner turmoil (though probably not all do). Some parents withstand emotional firestorms better than others, as the scale of differentiation would suggest. But of course they are the ones who have less of that sort of thing with which to contend, because their kids are also higher on the scale!

When the adolescent, increasingly in the adult world, does make mistakes, and all do, they will be bigger and more consequential mistakes. This adds to the family's anxiety level. The attractive and dangerous lures of a world in regression, another source of stress leading to anxiety in the family can quickly propel the family with an adolescent into emotional turmoil and chaos—a period some would rather not deal with at all. Intense relationship patterns and postures can emerge out of this time in the life of a family, adding to the problems.

Although the teen years have been characterized as a time of intense emotionality, this is not necessarily the case. The teenage years are not inevitably difficult or stormy. If parents' level of differentiation is high enough or at least being worked on and thought about, teenagers can go through these years with a minimum of inner turmoil, cutoff, rebellion, or other symptoms. Emotional maturity will be gradual, the rubber band phenomenon less perceptible.

This greatly desired outcome is not just a lucky break. Rather it comes about by parents working hard on managing themselves the very best they can in the family relationships. Of course, the parental level of differentiation will count for much. But even at very high levels of differentiation many stressors in a short time can raise the level of anxiety to the point that the functioning of the adults as mates and as parents is compromised.

At best parents may be bulldozed by the intensity of the emotionality and, sometimes, drama of their teenagers. At these times parents will be invaluable to each other if their own relationship is open and functioning well. They can help each other think through issues, gain objectivity, and get to calm rationality. And they can turn to friends, their own parents and siblings, and other parents for the experience they can contribute to add balance and grounding in a chaotic interval.

The National Institutes of Health study of adolescents, "Add Health," underscores the importance of parents' remaining intensely involved through the teenage years, even when they may think their role is diminishing. Richard Udry, one of the researchers says: "Many people think of adolescence as a stage where there is so much peer influence that parents become both irrelevant and powerless. It's not that parents aren't important. Parents are just as important to adolescents as they are to smaller children."

Ten Ways Parents Can Enhance Relationships with Teenagers

1. Listen

2. Stay calm when your teenager becomes emotional

3. Let your principles be known at appropriate times, in interesting ways, especially those having to do with relationships and relationship systems

4. Find enjoyable things to do together at least once or twice a month

5. Set and enforce your limits of what you can and cannot put up with

6. Celebrate any and every achievement, event, and milestone, even small ones; include the extended family whenever possible

7. Don't worry

8. Tell family stories

9. Keep the primary focus on you and your marriage (or adult relationships if you're a single parent)

10. Find ways to include the extended family in your family life

Murray Bowen exploded many myths—one of them concerned the teenage years. "A commonly held notion is that adolescence, the transition from childhood toward adulthood, is a stormy period. For the child with reasonable differentiation and secure parents, adolescence can be an exciting and adventuresome challenge, rather than a period of emotional turmoil."

Adult Offspring

As young adults, our offspring may be more like teenagers, but with time they mature. They eventually reach for and gain true adulthood. They will make their own mistakes, which will teach them a great deal. But over time they will have finished many important tasks of human existence begun in adolescence and even earlier. Their formal education will be completed, they will leave home and live independently, and they will choose mates and vocations. Their ethical stands will become somewhat definite. They have been launched. While they may show occasional dependence upon parents financially or in other ways, in general they have become independent adults—individuals. At that time the lifetime level of differentiation of self (level of basic self) is achieved. From that time on, if it is going to increase further it will take a lot of work.

It is at this point that our long goal of relationship equality with the next generation becomes actual. This shift, if never considered and prepared for, is one some parents never make. They can be heard saying things like, "To me you'll always be my little boy."

But if the goal of equality is kept from the beginning, gradually and step by step, some time in early adulthood a relationship equality emerges that is solid and useful to everyone. This equal posture in relationships, developed at home, carries over into all relationships, so that not only does the family benefit from the maturity of the new generation, but the world does as well. Parents who produce an independent, responsible adult who relates to them and others as a separate, open, and equal human being, achieve one of the foremost fulfillments in life.

When They Marry

Marriage of an adult son or daughter is most definitely a nodal event for a family. While a normal, natural fact of adult life, creating a new nuclear family can seem to be an event of landmark proportions. That new family means that someone, while remaining connected in important ways to his or her original family, in other important ways definitely leaves it. Both aspects represent tremendous change in lives in the family. The new family will have all the challenges of learning to live together, creating a new generation, while bringing the heritages of two families together. That is not an easy task.

The original family, meanwhile, experiences a great change. Fran Ackerman, a therapist and a mother, sees the triangles with one's child and his/her spouse as challenging. The shift occurring when a child marries can be striking and parents often experience an actual feeling of loss. But an awareness of these feelings and their predictability can help one to manage self in the relationships.

Sometimes parents learn principles of Bowen family systems theory relatively late. They can still put the ideas into practice up to the level of their understanding. If parent and offspring are in good enough contact, and the parent is working on his or her own level of differentiation, over time the relationships will flourish and eventually develop into a relationship of equals with self boundaries and openness. Everyone in the family will benefit by the effort.

Can flexibility and principles co-exist? From the time of gestation to adulthood, being the parent of a new generation demands a large repertoire of behaviors from us. The needs of a newborn are quite different from those of a young school-age child or teenager. The best parents know this intuitively. Many others do not, and, staying always the same, may do pretty well with some ages of their children but not well at all with others. High functioning parents seem able to rise to the challenge of their ever-changing and growing children as a way to develop more flexibility in self.

Ackerman points out that mammalian survival depends on the female's responsiveness to her young. As a result, mothers have the exquisite ability to perceive and respond to their young offsprings' needs. Thus, female mammals have a tendency to focus on others. As the offspring grows, he/she requires changing kinds of care that include freedom to become increasingly independent. "This developmental change requires a change in mothering—with the mother needing to focus less and less on her young. In some parent-child relationships this reduction in mother's focus on offspring and in the offspring's eliciting less attention does not develop appropriately. For example, a son does not develop independence appropriate to his age—the mother continues to focus on him with the father in the distant position."

In Jane Goodall's observations of the Gombe Stream chimpanzees, Flint's continued dependence on his mother Flo was such that he never really separated from her, though he was long past the age where that normally would have occurred. When Flo died, the other chimps made attempts to integrate him into the group but he did not. He died three weeks later in the same spot where his mother had died.

Katharine Baker, a consultant and teacher in family systems theory and a mother, finds it helpful for people to try to remember what was important to them when they were the age of the child at any given time, yet not assuming the child has the same interests, talents, and difficulties as they did at his or her age. He or she may be very different.

Pat Hyland, a therapist and a mother, talks about the job of being the parent of a teenager: "Children need parental care, support and encouragement. They also need their own space to grow, learn and mature. There must be a balance in providing enough of both. The task of parents of adolescents is 'to know enough but not know too much'; the task of adolescents is 'to let parents know enough but not too much.' Parents who have a family systems theory way of thinking to guide them can make better choices, being available but not interfering as their children mature and reach for adulthood."

In a time of societal regression, when anxious young people are attracted into running away, joining gangs, taking drugs, or having sex, some parents will have a harder time recognizing and remedying cutoff and other relationship postures. When the problems of a society in chaos complicate and frustrate everyday life, parents may have increasing difficulty in just finding time to be there.

But parents living on principle prioritize relationships. They create time and energy to be present and accounted for, thinking systems while being the best they can be in the relationships. This improves the parent-child relationship at any stage, decreasing problems and symptoms.

Discipline will vary at different ages and stages in its form. But a parent who is led by principle and knows clearly what he or she will and will not accept from children will have to discipline less. There will be less unacceptable behavior. Bowen put it this way: "The parent who moves toward differentiation has to know who he is, what he believes, and what he will do or not do in the full range of human situations. This is difficult when others are continually disagreeing and telling him what he should and should not do."

Regarding permissiveness, or lack of it, he said:

> The term 'permissive' is part of a dichotomy. It is not possible to think of 'permitting' someone to do something without implication of control or reservation about it. A parent in control of self has no

problems in "controlling" his family without the use of force, discipline, or punishment. He does not have to state rules and principles over and over. The child knows his boundaries, and he has a choice of exceeding them if he knows the consequences. A child who grows up in this kind of "freedom," in which primary parental energy is devoted to responsibility and discipline of the parents' own "selves," will automatically emulate most of the important parental values and beliefs.

The overall process of "differentiating a self" is remarkably consistent in all people. However, the separate steps are highly individual. My experience is in sharp contrast with the common notion that there is a right and wrong way to rear children.

The situation recalls a mother who said, "I listen to one expert and it sounds right, and then I see another authority who says something still different and that seems right. You are an expert. I am here for you to tell me the right way." A no-self, anxious parent can unwillingly pervert 'right' way into failure, and a more mature parent can take a 'wrong' way and make it work. The clear definition of convictions and beliefs by which one lives a life comes from within one's self as the result of an individual effort. This is in contrast to the amalgamated "we-ness" derived from joint or group consensus, which is more comfortable for the present, but presents complications "when the chips are down."

All the ages of human development make somewhat different demands upon parents. But repeated experience shows that the extended effort necessary to continue to develop a better version of self definitely makes a difference. Armed with a way of thinking that really applies, parents can find ways to live out what they believe, appropriately and flexibly at all the different ages and stages of their offspring.

The Single Parent and Combined Families

While two natural parents working together rearing the young is ideal, it doesn't always work out that way. Half or more of all families are now headed by single parents. Does family systems theory leave them out? Absolutely not! If anyone needs principles and guidelines, they do. Not only will theory help them navigate the white waters of a divorce, it also is there to help an individual or a family survive the deep water of the death of a spouse.

Divorce with Kids

When two people have built meaning and a daily life together (harder and harder to do in regressed times) they, their families, and all their friends may feel a great wrenching pain when they separate and divorce. That anxiety is intensified when the two have children.

Therapist and researcher Andrea Maloney-Schara defines divorce as "really just a legal agreement that grants some physical or emotional distance to two people who no longer understand each other." In the 1940s the average rate of divorce was 16 percent and now it is over 50 percent. She sees the increasing divorce rate as stemming from increasing relationship pressures owing to smaller nuclear families that are far more cut off from their extended families. She sees divorce as only one manifestation of a general tendency for wider family fragmentation.

Maloney-Schara believes that if we consider divorce as a communication problem between two people we miss the involvement we all have with the larger, past emotional systems. When people are willing to learn about these patterns of sensitivity, they learn to manage the emotional reactivity. If people can begin to understand how emotional process modulates anxiety in the system, they often become less blaming and judgmental of each other.

Many divorcing people, often children of cutoff, will not feel anything but positive feelings in the beginning—of the "I am so glad to be rid of you" variety. If they know of no way to make the relationship function better, they think they had better cut off and the sooner the better. This thought is more driven by feelings than logic, usually. For many of these "cutoffs," family theory will show a way to work on it and make it run better. Divorce becomes unnecessary, and they go on to a higher level of relationship functioning.

For those who seek the euphoria of the initial stages of cutoff in divorce, it is difficult to see how they might be making a mistake or how life could be anything but better without that troublesome other person. In time, however, the initial high wears off and anxiety (depression, physical symptoms, wild, crazy behavior) sets in. People do not connect this anxiety to the cutoff because of the good feelings initially imparted by the cutoff in the beginning. *The idea that the same trigger could instigate two different emotional states, one followed by another, is foreign to most of us but incredibly useful to realize.*

Divorces can be stormy, impulsive, vindictive, angry, hateful, harmful, frustrating, and hopeless. They can also be strung out, calm, passive, cooperative, reasonable, or quiet. As Edward Beal, author of *Adult Children of Divorce,* points out, "the divorce will most likely mirror the relationship style of the marriage. The same patterns, postures and impasses will come up." He finds that it is not divorce that makes a difference for children as much as the manner in which the parents divorce and the way a family organizes itself during and after the divorce. "Certainly differentiation levels make a difference in divorce, as in marriage."

With differences in differentiation come differences in communication with each other, attorneys, and with children. Some people have been known to find a way to separate and divorce without involving themselves in the triangle of attorneys, professionals who often have the effect of cranking up the already high intensity between the two.

Being open with children throughout the process, in ways appropriate for their ages and without triangling them in emotionally, is tricky. But children have a need to know what is happening in their family as it starts to take a different form. They will need to know something of the emotional problems that led their parents to take this step. They will need to know that their parents' problems are not their children's fault. And since there will be major change in their lives, they will need to know what these changes may be and what provisions will be made for them to have an ongoing relationship with each parent.

Dr. Beal believes that defining the family emotional patterns that led to a divorce and the part that each member played in it is the best post-divorce gift one can give to one's children. Children can do well if they can understand what happened to their parents' marriage and can extricate themselves from the family emotional processes.

For their own sakes, as well as those of the children, divorced parents will be better off not cutting off from each other but continuing their relationship in some way. At any rate, they will have to continue to be involved with each other in the rearing of their children so any work they can do with self to improve the functioning of the parental relationship will be of use to everyone. They can see this as a liability or as a challenge and opportunity—another arena in which to better their level of differentiation of self. This "pushing up" is always best done in the difficult relationships anyway, not the easy ones.

Death of a Parent

While families go through a great number and variety of feeling responses when a spouse and parent dies, they do not always follow the responses or the order of them listed in the well-known literature on death and dying. But, of course, there have to be pain and loss associated with this nodal event in a family's life.

How the surviving spouse/parent emotionally negotiates this tremendous loss will probably mean that he or she as well as the children will either "function up" or that the group will go on to a lower level of adjustment more or less permanently.

Watching some families going through the deep waters of death has been a privilege. Important efforts in their journeys to higher ground have involved conscious, deliberate attempts to stay in contact with the families of origin of the dead spouses/parents.

In the first case, with a fair amount of cutoff in the family, the surviving (divorced) mother called the dead father's family every day of the week leading up to the funeral to "walk them through" the events of each day. They were elderly and could not travel. This was the beginning of a more meaningful relationship with them. A further effort over ensuing years to "stand in" with them for their dead son was deeply appreciated by the grandparents. This meant special efforts for birthdays, vacations, and holidays. It also led to their grandchildren being better connected with them. Everyone benefited by this theory-guided effort.

In another family, where the father died leaving a wife, teenagers, and young adults, the surviving spouse found many ways to be connected with her dead husband's family, though they lived an ocean apart, requiring many phone calls and several visits both ways! This family, although experiencing loss and pain, did not go through the "classical" reactions to grief. Life resumed orderliness and productivity much more quickly than might have been predicted. The mother later remarried. The stepfather and his extended family have become acquainted with, like, and respect the family of the dead father. This has allowed for more flexibility and comfortable contact for all members, especially the young adult children whose father died. The mother states,

> We think of Joe often, missing him and remembering earlier times. Our three children are doing well, pursuing their own careers and goals. Communication is open with all extended family members. My husband knows Joe's extended family and they accept him. Theory and careful thinking helped us to get through difficult times and to move on despite our loss and sadness. These years and this family life transition has helped us be more thoughtful family members and stronger individuals, understanding more about both death and life. We today are in a better place because we were able to avoid pitfalls and unhealthy family patterns. Family systems theory is helpful in calm times but invaluable during periods of high anxiety and transition.

A dead spouse, after all, is not the whole unit, but a fragment of an emotional unit, some of which is still there, and available for contact.

When people understand and guide their living by theory, to the extent that they stay in touch with this extended family unit, they have a much different experience than what we often observe. They are, by staying in contact with the emotional unit of the dead person, preventing the cutoff that often accompanies the death of an important family member. *Is it possible, therefore, that the classic grief reactions described in medical literature are really more a reaction to cutoff than to death?* In the cases presented the survivors' reactions were very different, not because the person wasn't loved or missed but because the family stayed in contact with the emotional unit of which he was a part. In this way they avoided severe emotional reactions and dysfunction that really may have more to do with cutoff from an emotional unit than death itself.

Therapist, mother, and grandmother Janet Kuhn found in her research that regardless of whether the loss of a parent was from divorce or from death, the pain extends beyond the immediate loss of relationships. She found ongoing deprivation and heightened anxiety from added stress of living without the partner's help. Those who recover from a loss with the least impairment are those where the function of the lost parent is replaced either by remarriage or by the extended family taking over some of the duties of the deceased parent.

Single Parents

Having survived the death of a spouse or a divorce, there is still a lot of life to live and Bowen family systems theory can point the way for single parents as well as for married ones.

The quality of single parents' ex-spousal relationship will continue to carry an impact to their relationships with their children. What if the former spouse is married and the new spouse objects to the two parents making contact? It is still necessary and given time, experience shows the new spouse will usually adjust to the fact, necessity, and even advisability of the parents' relationship.

A single parent's family of origin and friendship system take on added importance and are absolutely vital to the best possible functioning of the single parent. They need to be given priority and can go a long way toward substituting for an on-the-scene spouse.

Friends and family can be invaluable to help get all the way through a problem when it can't be done alone. But it is impossible for someone else to do the thinking for one. This no-self position will wear everyone out.

Kids are a constant challenge and a lot of work, so a single parent needs time away—on vacation and just time out to go to dinner and see a movie, just as do married spouses. For most people, it is much more fun to go away with adult friends or family than alone.

Stepparents

Clinicians hear happy stories of adults whose stepparents, apparently accepting their jobs with enthusiasm and pleasure, made tremendous and positive differences in their lives. The negative step-parent experience is not by any means universal.

The stepparent has the very human (only rarely do we hear of other species rearing step-offspring) challenge of helping to rear individuals not genetically linked to them. But the human can, instead of thinking in negative terms, see the possibilities for contributing and enriching his or her own life as well as that of others in the family simultaneously. Many are the lives whose courses have been fundamentally altered by a stepparent who came into a family, becoming involved, interested, defining self, and being there in a positive way, making his or her unique contribution to the family.

Katharine Baker's work in the area of blended families is of interest. She has found that stepfamilies are like most other families except that the triangles are more intense. She notes that "remarriage following a divorce and period of single parenting often carries negativity from the first marriage and parent-child intensity from the single parent years." Following the death of a parent, she finds that "children can carry an idealization of the dead parent that makes it difficult for the new step parent to make any mistakes or just be a normal average person. De-mythologizing the dead parent can contribute to a more balanced relationship between the remarrying couple."

Dr. Baker encourages remarried couples to work on their relationships with former divorced spouses so that they can deal with each other directly as parents rather than through their children.

She points out that the larger extended family of children in blended families—they often have four sets of grandparents and innumerable cousins, aunts, and uncles—can be seen as an asset for them, rather than a liability.

In the beginning a stepparent is, emotionally, an outsider. But every position in a family has its positive aspects, even being on the outside. From this less emotionally crowded perspective one can take one's time and calmly look in on the system as it exists, just observing. One can gain an appreciation of its history, its weaknesses, and especially its strengths. In this way one can get ideas about the self in the new system and then determine what kind of relationships one wishes to develop—how one wishes to "be there." Seen as a great and important life contribution and project that will go on over time, there is no rush or forcing in this role. Rather, in a step-by-step process of living according to principle, one gets always closer to where one wants to be—with self and with the others. A stepparent, as any other parent, can make a tremendous impact by focusing on strengths and neglecting weaknesses.

Primary to making and improving relationships with the kids, of course, is a solid, well-functioning relationship in one's marriage, if remarried. The marriage is the emotional nucleus of the new family system or unit the two are trying to create. The couple will set the emotional climate and functioning level of differentiation at which the whole group operates. Out of that solid relationship emanates the interest, affection, and guidance toward youngsters that promote their best development. The children will not polarize this kind of a relationship. They will instead respect and cherish it. They will learn about marriage from it and look ahead to forming a relationship like this for themselves later on.

In blending two families or in marrying into an existing unit, parents cannot demand that everyone love everyone, neither stepsiblings nor a new step-parent. But good manners, friendliness, and respect can be expected, shown, and even overtly taught. This kind of parental leadership can go a long way toward promoting the high functioning that every parent wants to see, though relationships may not always go smoothly in the beginning. If these attitudes are maintained in the marriage they will flow naturally to the offspring.

Adopting Children

Adopted families are no different, from a theoretical standpoint, than others—all families form an emotional unit. No different, that is, until we begin to pin our hopes, dreams, worries, and other fantasies on the adopted children. Because they are adopted they may be sitting ducks for becoming the focuses of the family projection process. Instead of worrying and focusing them into anxious, symptomatic positions, if we can see them as separate and different individuals with a right and obligation to run their own lives, while keeping that connection with them, their chances for success will be greater.

Does a family planning to adopt want to include the birth parents in an ongoing way or not? Successful experiences are known to occur in both instances. Including birth parents in family life complicates life for the adoptive family in some ways, but not including them may represent cutoff of important potential relationships, with its attendant negative effects. Whether or not birth parents are included from the beginning, the author's impression is that, often, people sooner or later want to meet their birth parent(s). If this very common phenomenon can be a part of adoptive parents' thinking from day one the actual meetings will be smoother for everyone whether or not birth parents are included in the growing up years.

Does one tell a child he/she is adopted (some say "chosen")? Theory would seem to point the way toward openness in most situations. People can deal with realities better than whatever might be the alternative. If parents are accepting and comfortable with the circumstances of the adoption, marital communications function well, and if they have a satisfactory connection with their children, openness comes naturally and easily.

Carroll Hoskins, consultant, teacher of family systems theory, and mother, notes that adopted children, by virtue of their membership in at least four families, are imbedded in complex interlocking triangles. Families frequently use cutoff to try to manage difficult and painful relationships within these triangles. These cutoffs can contribute to increased anxiety, decreased sense of solid identity, and diminished functioning. She believes that adoptive families can define themselves in ways that will leave their children free to find ways to experience emotional connections in both their adoptive and biological families. "At times this may mean supporting one-on-one personal relationships. At other times this may mean facilitating objective awareness of biological, cultural, and emotional inheritances."

Anne Curran, therapist and mother, has also thought about adoptive families from a theoretical perspective. She believes that adoptive families are child-focused families. "There are many reasons people will give for adoption but the basis for most is to have and raise a child or children. There is a very broad spectrum of child focused activity in the parent/child relationship in adoptive families. In recent years one trend is of interest—grandparent adoptions. It seems to be an indicator of a regressed society where parents are unable or unwilling to care for their own offspring. In these sometimes highly anxious families the intensity of the grandparent, parent, child triangle is significant. Careful management of this triangle and likely involvement of lawyers and the court provide challenges at every turn."

She thinks that anxiety in adoptive parents as well as children is usually fairly intense and governs the process and the results for the family. Coaching from the beginning of adoption can help in establishing the new family unit.

An increasing number of our families are combined and many more headed by single parents because of the increase of divorce in this time of societal regression. But it is still possible to work on clarifying one's principles, and living life according to them, no matter what the situation.

Parents can learn from past and present relationships—successes and failures—by looking through the lens of theory. In this way they can usually manage to see a way of improving their important roles in family relationships, both with their spouses or significant relationship system and with the young as well. Principles of individual and family functioning will show them how to have better relationships with everyone in every type of family.

Play, Self-Regulation, and the Many Ways to Deal with Anxiety

Paul MacLean's work on the human brain showed that our brain is organized in a "triune" manner. For some functions, it is organized like that of reptiles. For other functions it is like that of other mammals, and for others (thinking and planning) it is uniquely human. A vital "paleo-mammalian" phenomenon found in that part of the brain, is that of play. Play with siblings assumes critical importance in development. Rough and tumble play, for example, is basic training for neuromuscular development. Play lays down the basics for social skills. It can teach how hierarchy works, since siblings are not usually the same age. It dissipates anxiety, at its best, in an explosion of good feelings. In some species adults are not observed to play. In others, including the human, play is a most important and useful part of life. When play is omitted or neglected, life is not in optimal balance.

Humor, a form of play, dissipates anxiety, restores perspective, and no doubt in this way readjusts brain chemistry. As a result of these changes, moods improve, energy increases, and people get along with each other more cooperatively. What a gift, humor!

Families coming for consultation about problems, asked about how much fun they have as a family, almost universally report they have none at all. With them play is a lost or never-developed art. Once they start playing together, "the problem" often does not last long.

The H Family

George and Mary H's oldest child, Tim, was on drugs, underfunctioning in school, and spending inordinate amounts of time with companions in similar straits, though they were, for the most part, all from high functioning families. George described intense conflict, alternating with distance with this son. Of course the focus on him was enormous because of his dangerous behavior that was so out of sync with the rest of the family.

In trying to plan a way to get back into a more positive kind of relationship with his son, George thought it would be through play. He planned several outings he thought Tim would enjoy. George's plans were rejected at first. Eventually Tim did accept an invitation to a sports event. That was the beginning of a turnaround in the relationship that, of course, involved much effort on George's part. But later both would point to the importance of having fun together as pivotal in their improved interactions with each other.

Phil Lorio, a family systems-oriented psychiatrist, reminds us that an ingredient essential to being an effective parent is developing a sense of humor about self and the stumbling, fumbling process called being a parent. "It is important for one's spouse and children to know one as a person who enjoys life and who looks for opportunities to laugh at self. Likewise, it's important to have a healthy, balanced recreational pattern in one's life, including an active social and friendship network in individual and family contexts. A regular pattern of entertainment and recreation for parents helps to renew and refresh their relationship so that they are able to develop and sustain an increased emotional flexibility and awareness of each other as well as the children."

Different families have different ways of having fun together. And, yes, it's sometimes a challenge to find activities that kids and adults can all enjoy. But they are there. Simple everyday practices such as walking together can catalyze openness in relationships—having fun does not have to cost money. Events like watching a sunset—free for the taking—are intensely pleasurable. The game "What do you see in that cloud?" is always there, as well as a hundred others like it.

The J Family

Louise J was not looking forward to the first Thanksgiving after her divorce. She was fairly distant, if not cut off, from her own family of origin so she needed to somehow get through the holiday with her two sons. She thought her best option would be to make reservations to eat out. She was definitely not up to cooking the feast. As the three got in the car to go she noticed her older son, Jeff, carrying a small book, but paid little attention. Walking into the restaurant she wondered if her depressed mood would allow her to get through the meal without crying.

While waiting for the food to arrive, Jeff pulled out his little book and began to read aloud from it. "Waiter, there's a fly in my soup!" he read. As he read the waiter's answers to a hundred different soups with flies, the little family was in stitches. They survived their first holiday without a dad and learned a very important lesson about creative kids and the uses of humor in the family.

Psychiatrist researcher Jerry Lewis's optimal families all evidenced humor and spontaneity.

Dr. Murray Bowen observed that "The human phenomenon is serious and tragic, but, at the very same time, there is a comical or humorous aspect to most serious situations."

We have considered something about how anxiety interferes with family relationships and functioning. That's where humor comes in—its great contribution to family emotional balance is its ability to dissipate anxiety, changing the mood from negative to positive quickly. And when anxiety is in abeyance, the relationships function better.

Just being in the presence of someone who is calm can lower the anxiety level to the point where the intensity for the whole family system is lessened. Also learning theory—reading about, thinking about, or trying to apply it with a coach—over time, will tend to reduce anxiety in the self, and thus, in the family unit.

Coaching

Psychotherapy, or coaching with a therapist trained in Bowen family systems theory, has a great number of advantages. If a child is symptomatic it can provide the turnaround that other therapies or simply reading a book cannot.

First, therapy can help the family system to reduce the anxiety to the point where it can begin to think with some reliability. Second, some objectivity from an outside neutral person can be invaluable in that thinking process. Third, although one can learn a certain amount of theory from a book, to actually apply theory to the living laboratory of life, a coach is indispensible. As people begin to take responsibility for their own emotionality, and handle it better, rather than merely passing it along the system, everyone functions better.

It is surprising to some families of symptomatic children that the therapist actually does the primary work with the parents. Sometimes the coaches do not even see the child more than once—sometimes not at all! That is because *parents themselves are the best coaches for their children.* Therapists actually have very little influence on them compared to that of their parents. By getting emotional intensity under control and anxiety resolved in the parents and the relationships working better, the whole family benefits.

This is not to say parents are to blame for children's problems. Certainly children play a part, as do the generations of intensity of the family. This symptom is merely the latest form the family intensity has taken. So while not to blame (the parents are doing the best they know how up to now) the parents can take responsibility for some changes in how they interact with each other and the whole family. If they do that, with a trained, experienced coach, everyone in the family can be expected to do better.

Training in Self-Regulation

Another invaluable aid in regulating anxiety within the self has come about in the last few decades as a result of the study of automatic processes in the body by means of electronic monitoring. It has been discovered that any physiologic function that can be brought to conscious awareness can be controlled consciously. The method used in this training is called biofeedback.

In the training, physiologic processes such as blood pressure, muscular tension, and other parameters of anxiety such as sweat response and hand temperature are monitored and brought into conscious awareness—"fed back"—to the person. In this way the feedback tells one how anxiety is being handled. Relaxation can be learned, and it is incompatible with anxiety. So, the better one becomes at relaxing, the better one is at handling anxiety.

Lilian Rosenbaum, therapist, researcher, mother, and grandmother, first developed the use of biofeedback with family theory-guided psychotherapy. In treating families she sees that there are many ways to work with a problem in the offspring. "Symptoms can be decreased in frequency, intensity and duration. Certain kinds of symptoms may not be possible to remove but it is possible to ameliorate them or manage them in such a way that they do not interfere with quality of life." She prefers to work with the parent(s) or responsible adults and coach them on how they can reduce their reactivity, increase their differentiation, increase the clarity of their "I positions" and communications to their offspring, while developing better understandings of their own places in their own multigenerational family systems. An important component of her work is to facilitate lower reactivity and increased functioning with psychophysiological monitoring, psychotherapy, and/or training.

Dr. Rosenbaum notes that "In treatment, avoiding injuring the amygdala by decreasing stress and sometimes changing prescribed medications is important." She also emphasizes improving health and nutrition.

Her treatment of the young can include a "productive focus" on the offspring, sometimes including psychotherapy, and sometimes with biofeedback training as appropriate for a specific symptom or for improved management of stress. The most important members of the health team for treating a youngster are the parents. She coaches parents to conceptualize and develop systems strategies early so as to prevent dysfunction, focusing less on treatment and more on wellness and high functioning.

Priscilla Friesen's work with biofeedback in families is interesting. It

is one way to see the way anxiety "moves" in the family. Measurements of the muscle tension, changes in hand temperature and sweat response indicate when an individual is reacting or becoming calmer.

When more than one member of a family is hooked up to the equipment at the same time, the patterns of anxiety or changes in the physiology of individuals can be observed. For example, when a mother and child are hooked up and the mother is complaining and worrying about the child, the physiology of the child is anxious or aroused and the mother's physiology is calmer. However, if the mother talks about or worries about herself, her husband, or her own mother in her child's presence, the mother's physiology becomes more reactive and anxious and the child's physiology is calmer.

More complex relationship patterns such as triangles can also be observed. With at least three individuals hooked up to physiological monitors, one can observe the subtle changes. For example, while measuring a husband, wife and husband's mother, the mother might make reference to her affection for her son. The son's physiology increases while the mother and wife calm down. This is an example of an anxious outside point in a triangle and the calmer inside twosome. These three individuals will all physiologically calm down when they talk about a fourth person.

These changes are happening all the time. When the anxiety is greater and the relationships more strained, one is more aware of the physiological markers of anxiety and can observe their movement through a system.

In a new generation of biofeedback technology, brain waves—the electrical activity the brain is constantly generating—can be monitored and brought into awareness. In this form of training, called electroencephalographic (EEG) biofeedback or neurofeedback, people are actually learning to modify abnormal or unwanted brain waves. A few of the conditions now being treated in this way include obsessive-compulsive disorder, attention deficit disorder, headache, head trauma, and even addictions.

Friesen, using this technology, can see how the

> brain of a child is connected to the brains of the parents. When any one of these brains change, it has an effect on the others. Patterns of the brain waves are reflections of the ways that a person has adapted in the relationships needed to survive effectively. So, when working with a child toward increasing his or her ability to focus, for example, one must consider the rest of the relationships.

There are problems when therapists agree with the family that the child is the problem. If one does EEG training under those circumstances, it can in fact set the problem in the child rather than seeing the child as an anxiety receptacle for the family. The broader picture is a more accurate one. The brain patterns developed in response to others'. When parents can be involved to see how these brain patterns are relationship patterns, the use of a tool such as neurofeedback is most effective. This might include one or both parents' using the neurofeedback for themselves. More importantly, it is the ability for the family to see more accurately the patterns of how anxiety is passed around in a family—and then, what one chooses to do about it.

Toward More Flexibility in Anxiety Management

The traditional therapy profession, in general, seems to know of only one way, other than drugs, to lower anxiety, and that is to "talk it out." This, in therapy, can sometimes be useful. (In family systems theory-guided coaching, *thinking it through* is even more useful.) But when talking it out is the only means people have for reducing anxiety, they often find themselves, with or without guidance from therapists, spilling anxiety into their friendship and family systems. Certainly there are times when one's family/friendship system can be invaluable in order to get to clarity, as we have already seen. But becoming an anxiety-generator in a system is not the best position for which to strive. Most relationships cannot tolerate people who continually dump their anxiety into the relationship.

Actually, there are many, many ways to reduce the anxiety level of the self, and thus, of the group. Calm is infectious, too. Let us consider just a few that trainees and workshop audiences have suggested. And this list is only a beginning. We can all make our own, and pull it out when needed. The brain may not think well enough at a time of anxiety to retrieve the items on the list unless it is committed to paper.

Thirty Ways to Reduce Anxiety

Here are some favorites:

1. Physical exercise of all kinds
2. Music
   - Listening to music
   - Making your own
3. Call or make contact with someone in your family—the idea here is mainly to make contact, not to "dump" anxiety
4. Call a friend—especially if you have one that understands Bowen family systems theory (wait until you are calm, however)
5. Arrange an event for friends
6. Think logically and through the lens of family systems theory about the problem. Thinking inhibits the emotional brain
7. Create or appreciate art
8. Go to a class, creating a new or nurturing an old interest
9. Get outdoors in nature—a show that's free for the taking
10. Care for, play with, walk, and/or talk to your pets
11. Garden, either indoors or out
12. Travel
13. Groom or maintain yourself, your family, your clothes or other possessions
14. Look for the bigger picture
15. Pray
16. Take up a new activity
17. Read (not only instructs but inhibits the emotional brain by activating the thinking brain)
18. Write letters, in journals, or for publication, or contact a cut-off branch of your family
19. Learn about your family's genealogy, with family systems principles in mind
20. Make the situation triggering your anxiety into a research project
21. Get active in any way that appeals to you. Activity dissipates anxiety
22. Shop for a new outfit or something for your home
23. Volunteer for a cause

24. Count your blessings—this one will turn a mood around very fast!

25. Make one-, five-, and ten-year plans for your life in various areas such as relationships, finances, and vocation, and divide these into steps to be taken. Take one of them now!

26. Encourage or lend a hand to someone

27. Count to ten slowly

28. Take deep, slow breaths

29. Relax your muscles

30. Keep on keeping on with your daily routine, putting one foot in front of the other. Remind yourself that feelings come and feelings go

Everyone can add their own personal thirty more ways of reducing the anxiety level!

Music and Anxiety

Michael Sullivan, a family theory consultant and a musician, talks about music:

> Music produces sound waves that stimulate electrical and chemical activity in the brain. By engaging the autonomic, feeling and thinking systems, this stimulation activates the full range of human feeling, thinking and action states. Subjectively, music triggers memories of past relationships and life events or fantasies about current ones. The function of music is equivalent to play as either a rehearsal for current life situations or a reenactment of the past. It can diminish anxiety and provide a sense of mastery over powerful emotion or increase anxiety by triggering memories of past heartbreak and loss. It represents the highest level of human invention, yet activates the most infantile memories and feeling states.

> Parents and teenagers frequently disagree about what constitutes music.

> The type of music that becomes popular provides some indication of society's level of functioning. The themes of alienation, togetherness and individuality in music reflect the balance of regressive and progressive forces within the society that produces it. Every type of music has an audience.

Parents who understand something about anxiety and have a large number of ways of managing it in self have a definite advantage in relationships and in all of life. If anxiety can be calmed in some way, the trigger(s) for it will usually be identified and dealt with appropriately. These parents will lead their families to higher functioning, with fewer symptoms. They are also in the admirable position of being able to teach their children what they know about anxiety and its management in relationships and in life.

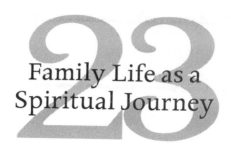

Family Life as a Spiritual Journey

The idea that there is more to human existence than what we experience with our senses—and a part of us that lives on after death—is universal. Spirituality, while not a formal concept of Bowen family systems theory at this time, is ubiquitous in human society. Freud looked for explanations of the human interest in the spiritual, which to many served to explain it away. Many of those who tried to live life without a belief in someone/something greater than self, found life to be less rich, less calm, and less full of meaning. This belief in transcendence is reflex for many people during times of anxiety or during nodal events in the life of a family, such as births, marriage, and death. These evoke an intense sense of meaning. At these times people often reach for a spiritual meaning intrinsic to human existence. Considering life from a spiritual perspective is tremendously enriching and a great resource for some families.

Peggy Treadwell developed a counseling center in a large city church. She notes that "It is within the context of our families that each of us develops an intellectual, emotional, physical and spiritual self. This development is a lifelong task, and journey is the most useful metaphor to describe the process."

She equates this with development of the soul in a creative way. "Clearly, families can create an atmosphere to foster this development or hinder it. Ideally, in the family, we can grow to our fullest potential, be in contact with an intense emotional system while defining self, acting with and for others without being selfish or selfless."

Parents with a strong religious or spiritual faith, Treadwell believes, often say, "my children are God's children only lent to this family for a brief time. I turn my children over to God's care and protection many times during a day and night." She thinks that "These parents who understand God as in the process of their family life are less invested in the outcome of their work as parents and more present to be with and accept their children as they are. This prayerful form of letting go may significantly reduce anxiety so that children can think and act more creatively, their spirits freer to connect with self, others and God on their spiritual journey."

Janet Kuhn puts it this way: "To be truly human is to be in part spiritual. People experience awe and ecstasy when a new being enters our world, referring to the miracle of birth. But nothing is more natural than birth. Through the entire life cycle of every individual and every family each stage of development gives way to the next and each brings its precious moment for the renewal of every family member. Who, attending a wedding does not remember his or her own promises to a spouse? Being spiritual is to be truly human; the difficulties and problems of family life can keep us focused on the mundane, but family life is also a natural growth path. In birth and death, in joy and in sorrow, we confront and can celebrate being."

Alcoholics Anonymous group support programs, and other twelve-step programs patterned after AA for people with addictions of various types, base their work on a belief in a higher power, however that may be interpreted by the individual. Their statistics for recovery have traditionally been some of the best in the field.

The Bowery Mission, a faith-based agency in New York City, also works with addicted people. Their statistics for recidivism, in five year follow-up studies have far exceeded those in non-faith-based agencies.

Psychiatrist David Larson, in combing the results of psychiatric studies in journals found that non church attenders are four times more likely to end life in suicide than church attenders. Religious involvement also protected adolescents and others against drug abuse, tobacco and alcohol abuse. Dr. Larson found reports that the religiously committed enjoy a greater sense of overall life satisfaction, lower rates of depression and much lower stress levels than do the less-committed. He also found lower levels of juvenile delinquency, greater levels of marital happiness and satisfaction with sex in marriage in religiously observant people than in the non-observant.

Families do seem to do better when they have spiritual resources than when they do not. Also, people often seem to become interested in spiritual possibilities once their nuclear and extended family relationships begin to get on course. This needs further study but the phenomenon has been observed by other professionals in the family field.

Of course, religion can be used for building purposes (building of self) or in the service of symptoms and regression. It is not unusual to have schizophrenic delusions take a religious form. And of course, some of the most difficult interlocking triangles take place in churches.

But prayer can be an instant anxiety reducer. It is always and instantly available. It is vital to the believer and a part of every known spiritual pathway. Singing and music, so much a part of many religious traditions, have an antianxiety value of their own.

The community of faith in a church, synagogue, mosque, or spiritual group can represent a resource for families. Ideally it does not supplant the nuclear or extended family but rather supports and enhances it.

Religious training cannot give one principles—they can only be gained by the hard work of thinking and trial and error. But the precepts or teachings of a religious tradition can serve to get one started in that hard work. They can't really become a part of the self until they are thought through all the way and put into practice in life. C. Margaret Hall, professor, writer, therapist, mother, and grandmother, is especially interested in values and emphasizes that "the value choices family members make influence how they relate to self, each other and to their communities. Spiritual or religious thinking may play a significant part in helping them to define their values."

Differentiation of self almost inevitably means defining oneself vis a vis the faith of the family of origin. A thoughtful approach to beliefs of the family may result in believing all that one has been taught. Or one may come out differing in some ways, or radically, from what one was taught. Defining oneself to one's family about one's faith can create anxiety in families who think everyone should believe the same thing or else there has been failure. But all of this is a part of differentiation of self, is it not?

Edward Beal tells parents who worry whether their children will grow up to be religious or spiritual or whether they will choose the same religion as they did, that family life itself is a spiritual journey. He thinks that "family emotional patterns can account for how children receive and accept the faith of their fathers and mothers. Because of that, working to clarify the family emotional patterns is an important way to give children the best opportunity to freely choose a religious and spiritual life."

Regressions in society have sometimes suppressed religion altogether as in the Soviet Union or have prohibited religious freedom, narrowing the choice to a state religion. But the inner spiritual devotion of the believer has never been entirely thwarted in history.

Parents aiming for better and better functioning in their families can use the time of regression as an opportunity to get closer to their spiritual resources, however defined. The regressive tendencies in society can actually be seen in their wider spiritual context, and as an opportunity to stand on principle, even if seemingly alone. There is an individuality in each of us that can identify whatever is conducive to higher and better functioning, especially including personal faith.

On Being a Self
in the Generations

I f there is any one key to becoming more nearly that high functioning parent we would all like to be, it is *staying in emotional connection with the generations of the family we grew up in and being, increasingly, over time, a self there.* To the degree that one can stand a little more apart from the emotional process in which one was reared, being more the self one wants to be, it is more possible to be separate and the best one can be in the nuclear family one has created also. It is virtually impossible to be cut off from one's family of origin and still function well as a parent.

Where there is cutoff, therefore, it becomes a high priority to bridge that cutoff. That bridging process in itself may take years. After that it's time to see what kind of work remains to be done *on self* in those relationships. It seems that many people heard what Bowen said about going back to your family of origin. Few seem to have heard what he said to do when you got there. For that reason, many have gone to their original families preaching, teaching, or therapizing. The point of going there is none of that. It is, rather, *to get in better connection and to become more of a self.*

This work we do on self, becoming more of a self in the family we grew up in, is of primary importance in the kind of job we do as parents. Katharine Baker has found the open, connected relationship that parents form with their own parents to be the most important work they do. This prevents their getting into the common pattern of trying to raise their children either the same way or the opposite way from the way they were raised. She further notes that "being in contact with one's own parents will give perspective and perhaps even calm when one approaches one's own child."

This kind of work on raising the functioning of the self in the family of origin has taken many forms in thousands of families, but the effort is always planned, guided, and carried out with theory in mind. Reading books and attending lectures and workshops is useful but personal coaching is probably essential for a serious effort. Sometimes the results can be astounding.

On Growing a Self in One's Family of Origin

Victoria Harrison, consultant, mother, and grandmother, describes the process of understanding the family emotional process in the generations.

> The implications for change are profound. When one can understand and alter one's own reactivity to past generations, there is far more choice in life. This is not a passive process of gaining insight, or of 'dredging up the past.' This is a process of gaining knowledge and putting it into action to change self in relation to the family. Marriage is a good example. Two people who have little contact with their parents, siblings, or other family end up reacting to each other as if the marriage contains all of the emotional reality. If one of them can put energy toward establishing contact with his or her family, the emotional process will come alive there, leaving the marriage more free to be an open, alive personal relationship between two mature individuals more of the time.

> The same thing happens with the focus on problems in the children. People who distance from difficulties with their parents or family, become over-focused on problems in other areas of life. One person can actually change the impact of the past on his or her life through this effort to understand more and be less reactive to the generations of one's family. Those of us who are parents and grandparents will be able to see the extent to which that effort changes things for future generations. There is evidence to suggest it is possible to make a difference.

Andrea Maloney-Schara emphasizes the great importance of staying connected in our extended families: "Common sense tells us that family relationships are important in rearing children. If fragmentation appears to be the most universal difficulty families face then one principle-oriented solution would be to get to know as many members of one's extended family as possible.

"In a coaching relationship people can often understand their place in the multigenerational family. Even if the family is filled with tensions, motivated individuals are able to see the old relationship triangles with less love or hate."

One Mother

When one mom began hearing and learning about the principles of Bowen family systems theory she was in psychoanalysis, being treated for depression she had been fighting for eight years. The new ideas immediately made sense to her. She stopped her analysis and began to be coached in the principles of the new-to-her theory. The first concept she understood was that of cutoff. She began to work on her cutoffs in her family of origin. This included reconnecting with her parents and her in-laws, with whom she had been emotionally cut off for eight years. The depression disappeared overnight never to reappear.

The reconnection was not the same as differentiation of self, however, although it was a beginning step. Further efforts, over several years, would include many trips back to her family of origin where she would continue the connections and move them to ever better levels of "friendship," as she came to think of it. In the beginning she would simply attempt to stay in the family home without distancing into sleep, reading, or physical symptoms of allergy or asthma. These were patterns of her childhood.

Later she would find ways to be more open with her beliefs, even though they might differ at times from those of her parents. By now her parents, far from being cut off, were valuable allies and resources in her own family dilemmas. Still later, stymied in an important personal goal or pursuit she was to find that unless she could be open and candid with her family, enlisting their empathy and support, she would remain stuck. Such is the power and connectedness of the family system!

Consultation in Bowen Family Systems Theory

By now it is evident that family systems theory provides a set of cohesive ideas that, at once, describe how people relate in groups—especially family groups—and also serve as guiding principles for functioning better in relationships. Much can be learned from books, but not enough. Most serious students of theory will want to obtain some coaching or consultation in the principles to see how they apply to life—their own lives.

Coaching that is oriented to the new way of thinking, that sees the family as a unit, differs from traditional therapy in some interesting ways. If one sees the family as an emotional unit then it is unnecessary to have more than one coach per family—in fact, it is contra-indicated.

Also, coaches/consultants often do not see children in the family, even if they may be the symptom-bearers. Most children have no interest in sitting around talking to an adult anyway, and gain little from the arrangement. The coaching is for the strength of the family, the parents. They are the ones who can change the emotional patterns in the family. Children, after all, really have very little power to do anything about the source of the problem—the unresolved relationship issues between the parents, and the emotional climate in the home. But they are very responsive to the changes their parents make. As the parents work on relating differently and better, children lose their symptoms. *Parents are the best "therapists" for children and no one else can do their work for them.*

One of the first jobs of the coach, or consultant, with a "new" family is to help them find a way or ways to lower their anxiety so they can think, listen, and respond to each other more thoughtfully. Once they can begin to think instead of just react, a bigger picture and new ways of being and becoming can emerge. They will start to solve their own problems.

From then on it is a matter of learning to know and apply a theory that either is, or is not, true to life. Their experience will tell. After the anxiety level decreases and people begin to think, people engage in the fascinating project of differentiating a self. This happens as they apply theory in day-to-day challenges in their nuclear families and in their families of origin, as well as in the workplace.

Many are so cut off that the first step with families of origin is just to make contact and then develop some relationships. Opportunities to connect with family at occasions such as reunions, funerals, or weddings are good as gold. Family diagrams are created and developed with the help of family members and genealogical study.

Thousands of families by now attest to the worth of a new and different way of thinking about human interactions. The more they learn, the more they apply what they know. The more they apply what they know, the higher their functioning in relationships and in their families. As this goes on coaching becomes less and less necessary because the theory is there to be the guide.

Grandparents

Now your work is done—you've raised your kids and they already have theirs. Maybe you can now sit back and rest, stopping all the effort—or can you? Well yes, you can, but your life will probably be shortened and certainly less meaningful and rich if you take that route.

The relationships with your adult children are enduring and will always take effort, thought, and connectedness. So whatever it takes to be there in the family you created, as it goes on in time, will be a high priority. Once those children have children of their own, and you are a grandparent, you have a new role.

The grandparent relationship is just beginning to get the study it has always deserved. Let's think about a few of the many functions of grandparents. Grandparents are a stabilizing force.

Suomi found that in his colony of research monkeys, grandparents moved in when mothers became tired, relieving them in that way. He also saw them as a calming influence in the group.

Katharine Baker studied families in Russia, in cooperation with Moscow State University. She looked at the impact on grandchildren of losing contact with grandparents. In the Soviet Union, many people lost their grandparents prematurely because of Stalin's "purge." The main finding of the study was that grandchildren who really know their grandparents in a personal way (or at least know a lot about them through their parents if the grandparents are dead), do better in their adult lives than grandchildren who don't have a good sense of who their grandparents are/were. This means that they are healthier, have fewer physical and psychological symptoms, and fewer divorces, and their own children do better in school. The study was limited to people growing up in the Soviet Union during the 1950s and 1960s, but the assumption is that the findings are applicable to any population.

Two different families who rent their vacation homes to other families have noted that when grandparents are present on the vacation the behavior of families is different. When they are present the owners can count on orderliness, and there will be no damage to the property or furniture. The difference, both owners reported, was striking and reliable over years of time.

Fran Ackerman notes that "Grandchildren introduce new triangles into the family. For example, an intense triangle of grandmother, daughter-in-law and grandchild can interlock with another of grandmother, son and daughter-in-law." She notes that "as children become parents it is an arena in which one can further develop adult-to-adult relationships."

Janet Kuhn's thoughts on being a grandparent are useful.

> Other things being equal, that of grandparent is probably the most enjoyable relationship that one can have. It must be universal—people always refer to having all the pleasures and none of the responsibilities of children. The intensities, worries and concerns of the parent/child relationship are not present. For this reason grandparents can be a great resource for parents and children alike. The generation span allows a grandparent to be less invested in outcomes involving the grandchildren and thence gives more opportunities just to enjoy experiences. They can help in tangible ways such as baby sitting and financial help. But the most important aspect of being a grandparent is giving children an expanded relationship system that enhances their experiences with family.

> The quality of the relationship between grandparent and grandchildren depends in large part on the kind of relationship that exists between grandparent and parent. If there is tension in that relationship it will spill over to the children and sometimes they get caught in the middle of unresolved conflicts. It is then the task of the grandparent to work on self and the unresolved issues in one's family of origin.

C. Margaret Hall states:

Clinical work and research suggest the critical importance of participating in constructive three-generational interactions to improve family well-being. Grandparents are crucial players in increasing the openness and balance of their families, and in ensuring the sound development of their grandchildren or other members of the youngest generation. Grandparents make a real difference to the ways in which family members relate to each other, and they can start changes in their families and in their communities which will have a lasting impact on the next generations. Grandparents' participation in families and communities also reduces problematic conditions in overly rigid traditional families, families in conflict, dysfunctional families, emotionally and geographically distant families, fragmented families and blended families.

Meaningful, alive relationships between all the generations in the family become important and indispensable resources for all of us as we continue our efforts toward becoming the most effective parents and grandparents we can be. We need families of our own to turn to when the difficulties of life emerge. The grandparents need the connection with the young to stay alive and oriented to the future as well as the past and present. One effective way for grandparents to connect is to tell grandchildren stories about their parents growing up. They usually love to hear them.

Societal regression seems to pull family relationships apart—partly from the sheer effort it takes just to survive as a family group in the regressive times. It robs parents and children of the time needed for contact between and among family members to keep the relationships on course.

Parents and grandparents working on differentiation and higher functioning stay on course in spite of the troubled times by thinking systems, and:

- By being an individual and not being afraid to let one's thinking be known in the family
- By staying in contact. Though more of a task once the offspring are grown and not necessarily near home base, it is of primary importance if the extended family system is to be there for its members.

The tendency to segregate people as they age into communities of their own may be part of the regression—cutoff in society—and may need to be thought through again. This isolation of the aging generation deprives us all of the wisdom attained by experience and emotional grounding it can represent for us. Also, when the older generation is less accessible, it is less available for giving in all the ways that only extended family can. Similarly, the elders are deprived of the opportunity to be in better contact with family, with all its generations as well as with the wider community.

The Family in the Community

Dr. Hall has studied the relationship between the family and the wider society. She emphasizes the need for families to involve themselves with the community. Dr. Hall has discovered that "Making contributions to communities and society has an empowering impact on family functioning, just as improving family well-being has a constructive effect on communities and society. It is important to raise children, grandchildren, nieces, and nephews to think beyond their immediate family needs, as well as to take their family responsibilities seriously." In one study she found that the more families were involved in their communities, the better their functioning.

Jerry Lewis, in his study of optimal families, found that they were very much involved in the community.

Most societies have recognized the pivotal place of families to the wider community. The ancient Chinese called the family the basic unit of society. As goes the family so goes the whole society.

What happened to the little boy who could not learn, the one we followed in the beginning from learning problems on to conduct problems and substance abuse?

Since Johnny is only part of a much larger whole, his nuclear family and also his extended families, we must ask not only what happened to him but also what about his family?

His mother remarried and when that marriage began to fail she sought out a Bowen family systems trained therapist. As she looked at herself in her family she realized that she had been cut off from her family for several years. Following her therapist's promptings she began to work on her cut-off relationships in her family. The depres-

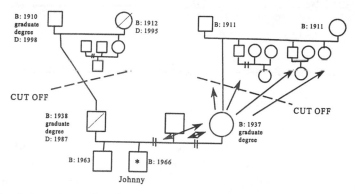

As Johnny's mother bridged her cutoffs, establishing new connections in her family of origin and defining herself there over time, she was able to establish relationships with her sons that had transformational effects.

sion she had carried for many years and despite several therapists' best efforts disappeared virtually overnight. With her new-found energy she then turned her attention to her relationships with her ex-husband, Johnny's father, and her two sons. Over time she saw the relationship with her ex-husband improve. He, too, went on to a second divorce. Shortly thereafter he became ill and died. Johnny's behavior went from bad to worse and his mother found it hard to stay connected with him. For many long months she did not know where he was.

Her premise was, however, that if she could get a connection with her son, the underachieving, irresponsibility, and substance abuse would disappear. Thus, she kept working away at getting a connected relationship with him while at the same time she worked on improving still further her relationships with her family of origin. It seemed that the more connected she became with her own family of origin, the easier all her relationships became.

The day came when, indeed she was able to make that connection with Johnny. Mother and son worked their way through many difficulties—with the law, with education, and with vocation. Her guiding principles included keeping a connection that would be open, equal, and with separate boundaries, hearing her son, and at the same time, when appropriate, not hesitating to define self—bringing her principles into the conversation.

For his part, Johnny became increasingly willing over time to hear what his mother was saying. Sometime during this process they became friends. Out of this friendship came exactly what her guiding premises had predicted. Johnny's attitude and life direction changed. Addiction and rebellious behavior dropped out. He never stopped being fun-loving, but in addition he now took on responsibility and integrity. He learned to go to work and be on time, giving the best of himself he could.

As a less anxious person, he could learn. School was now possible and although he was a little older than some of the students, he tackled it, did well, and is now planning to finish college and earn a professional degree.

His mother continues to work on relationships according to her guiding family systems principles. She often reminds herself of the importance of this and working on one's own differentiation level rather than focusing on others. She often wonders where they would be without the ideas that took her to a very different level in relationships and in so many other areas of life.

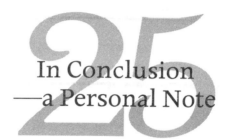

In Conclusion
—a Personal Note

We have taken a thought journey together in the fascinating territory of Being a Parent. We have seen how:
  - our society is in trouble,
- we, as families, are in trouble owing not only to society's trouble but also to our own immaturity, and
- children develop symptoms in the context of the family emotional system.

We have looked at a unique set of principles regarding the human family that:
- sees the family, not the individual, as the emotional unit—an idea that changes the way we see everything human,
- shows how one person, becoming more of a self, affects the entire family in emotional maturity, general health, and ability to do better in life,
- emphasizes relationships between parents, and between parents and their children as key to how children develop and what kind of adults they will be, and
- stresses the importance of connectedness of the generations.

We have seen what efforts of high functioning parents look like in some detail, and how using the new guidelines helps them to:
- observe more accurately,
- think more clearly, and then,
- take more useful and effective action—action based on principle.

I have often pointed out that Bowen theory is a theory about how people interact in groups. Fully seven of the eight formal concepts are explicitly about group interaction. Only one—differentiation of self—is concerned with the individual. But even that idea of the self is described in terms of relationships! So the self can only be understood in terms of its interactions with other people. This perception of the group as the emotional unit is very new to most people and stands in extreme contradistinction to traditional theory, only concerned with the individual, leaving out the bigger picture.

Most people who want to go further will need resources. *Extraordinary Relationships.* (R. Gilbert, John Wiley & Sons, Inc., 1992) goes into some of the relationship aspects of theory in more detail.

Other resources, though not exhaustive, can act as a springboard. Most parents who are interested in sibling position will want to refer to Dr. Toman's original writing. His book, as well as others written by Bowen, his faculty, and some trainees, is listed in Appendix 1.

Since theory cannot be learned outside the crucible of human experience and application, serious readers will want to find a coach or consultant (the best word has probably not been found at this writing). For those people there is a list of consultants in Appendix 2. If these do not work out in a specific instance they may have trainees of their own programs or know of others, not listed, that can be useful.

The Georgetown Family Center, founded by Bowen and his faculty, where a great deal of his professional activities were centered during much of his career, is in Washington D.C. It exists to promote, extend, and refine Bowen family systems theory by all of its numerous educational, research, and clinical functions. It has spawned many other centers, some of which are in Chicago, Pittsburgh, Princeton, Northern California, Houston, Kansas City, Vermont, Minneapolis, Tulsa, Memphis, and Florida.

Dr. Murray Bowen, days before his death, said, to an audience, "You have inherited a world of tribulation—take it and do the best you can with it." I think he was talking about the regressive society we are living in.

The only way I know to affect the regressive tendencies of society is for high-level people, with a knowledge of family systems principles, to rear their families according to what they know about relationships

and less along the lines of reactivity or the dictates of the regression. From these families, leaders could emerge with an interest in leading civilization up and out of the regression. They would know that the problems that have been created by humans can be solved by humans. They could find solutions based on principle rather than on anxiety. They would teach about staying on course instead of giving in to the ever-present regressive forces. This book is one effort to contribute toward that possible outcome.

Notes

Chapter 1

Statistics regarding societal regression are quoted from *The Index of Leading Cultural Indicators* by William J. Bennett, published jointly by Empower America, Heritage Foundation, and Free Congress Foundation.

Drugs as a leading industry are documented in Joseph Douglass, *Red Cocaine: The Drugging of America & The West,* Edward Halre, Ltd., New York, 1999.

Drug usage underestimate study is found in the *Journal of the American Medical Association,* Feb 26, 1992, "High Prevalence of Recent Cocaine Use and the Unreliability of Patient Self-report in an Inner-city Walk-in Clinic."

Statistics regarding teenage substance use and sexuality are quoted from a press release regarding "The largest adolescent study ever," "Add Health," reported in the *Journal of the American Medical Association* Sept. 9, 1997.

Califano quote from a press release re: address to Heritage Foundation Jan. 29, 1997.

Chapter 3

ADD and ADHD ideas by David E. Drake, D.O., Associate Professor of Psychiatry at University of Osteopathic Medicine and Health Sciences in Des Moines, Iowa. Reported in paper at Private Professional Day, Georgetown Family Center, October 30, 1996.

Daniel Papero and Robert Felton reported on regressive conditions affecting schools in a Professional Lecture Series lecture at Georgetown Family Center in 1997.

Substance use and school security measures reported in 1995 *Annual Report,* the National Center on Addiction and Substance Abuse at Columbia University.

Chapter 4

Effects of marijuana and risk behaviors reported in the 1995 *Annual Report* of the National Center on Addiction and Substance Abuse at Columbia University.

Michael Sullivan's studies reported in several conferences at Georgetown Family Center over several years.

Ann Bunting's thoughts on triangles between families and correctional facilities presented at Private Professional Day, Georgetown Family Center, October 30, 1997.

Chapter 10

See Helen Fisher, *Anatomy of Love,* New York, Norton, 1995, for the best explication of emotional and chemical bonds in couples.

John Calhoun's work on overpopulation and its effects on parental functioning reported in lectures at Georgetown Family Center by Roberta Holt.

Bowen's description of shock wave phenomenon in *Family Therapy in Clinical Practice* by Murray Bowen, Aronson, Northvale, N.J., 1985, p. 326.

Tessa Smith is quoted from her lecture at Georgetown Family Center Professional Lecture Series, March 19, 1997.

Chapter 11

Selden Illick has presented papers on cutoff at Georgetown Family Center conferences.

Andrea Maloney-Schara has presented several papers on divorce at conferences at Georgetown Family Center.

Bowen quote from a manuscript on an interview for *Marriage Magazine* by Arthur Ciervo.

Chapter 12

Kathleen Kerr's work from many lectures and presentations of papers at Georgetown Family Center, Washington D.C.

Bowen quote from a manuscript on an interview for *Marriage Magazine* by Arthur Ciervo.

Chapter 14

Eileen Gottlieb has reported her long-term study of survivor descendants of the German holocaust in several papers at conferences at Georgetown Family Center.

Chapter 15

Walter Toman's groundbreaking discoveries about the effects of family constellation and sibling position are set out in detail in *Family Constellation*, Springer Publishing Co., New York 1961, 1969, and 1976. Chapter 12 is especially pertinent for parents.

Chapter 16

Joseph Campbell's work on the ideas of leaders affecting society rather than society affecting them, reported in PBS Series by Bill Moyers on Joseph Campbell.

Yankelovich's polls reported in the *Index of Leading Cultural Indicators* by William J. Bennett, published jointly by Empower America, Heritage Foundation, and Free Congress Foundation.

Roberta Holt has reported on John Calhoun's work in numerous lectures at Georgetown Family Center. Calhoun's work is also reported in his own publications such as (with Pines): "How the Social Organization of Animal Communities Can Lead to a Population Crisis Which Destroys Them." (National Institute of Mental Health: Mental Health Program Reports—5: DHEW Publication No. (HSM)72–9042 December 1971: p. 158–173.)

Chapter 18

Bowen quote from a manuscript on an interview for *Marriage Magazine* by Arthur Ciervo.

Jerry Lewis's study of normal families is reported in *No Single Thread* by Lewis, Beavers, Gossett, and Phillips, Brunner Mazel, New York, 1976.

Chapter 19

Connectedness between parents and children reported most important antirisk factor in "Add Health," on adolescent health reported in the *Journal of the American Medical Association* Sept. 9, 1997.

Chapter 20

Myron Hofer's descriptions of prenatal influences on behavior are in *The Roots of Human Behavior,* Freeman and Co. New York, 1981, Chapter 10.

Paul MacLean's work on mammalian vocalization in *The Triune Brain in Evolution* Plenum Press, New York, N.Y. 1990, Chapter 21.

John Rosemond quote on TV-watching in "The 5 Point Discipline Plan for Raising Great Kids" in *Parent's Digest,* Fall/Winter 1998–99, p. 84.

Connectedness between parents and children important to teenagers, reported in "Add Health," on adolescent health reported in the *Journal of the American Medical Association,* Sept. 9, 1997.

Bowen quote from a manuscript on an interview for *Marriage Magazine* by Arthur Ciervo.

Parental demands for problem kids—idea in *How to Get Your Kids to Do What You Want Them to Do* by Paul Wood, Prentice-Hall, Inc, Englewood Cliffs, N.J., 1977.

Jay Barrish, in personal coaching, introduced the author to behavior modification techniques.

Chapter 22

Paul MacLean's work on play can be found in *The Triune Brain in Evolution,* Plenum Press, New York, N.Y. 1990, p.16.

Jerry Lewis's study of normal families is reported in *No Single Thread* by Lewis, Beavers, Gossett ,and Phillps, Brunner Mazel, New York, 1976.

Chapter 23

Larson, David, MD, MSHP, and Mary A. Greenwold Milano, BA, "Are Religion and Spirituality Clinically Relevant in Health Care?" Decker Periodicals 1995. This article is al good summary of much of Dr. Larson's work. Other publications by Dr. Larson can be obtained from National Institute for Healthcare Research, 6110 Executive Blvd. Ste 908, Rockville, MD, 29852

Chapter 24

Jerry Lewis's study of normal families is reported in *No Single Thread* by Lewis, Beavers, Gossett and Phillps, Brunner Mazel, New York, 1976.

Appendix 1

Reading Resources

Beal, Edward, and Gloria Hochman: *Adult Children of Divorce,* Delacorte Press, New York, 1991.

Bowen, Murray: *Family Therapy in Clinical Practice,* Jason Aronson, New York, 1978. A collection of Bowen's papers.

Family Systems, A Journal of Psychiatry and the Natural Sciences, Georgetown Family Center, 4400 MacArthur Blvd., Washington, D.C., 20007, 202–965–0730.

Gilbert, Roberta: *Extraordinary Relationships, A New Way of Thinking About Human Interaction* John Wiley & Sons, Inc., 1992. A guide to the use of Bowen family systems theory to improve relationships.

Hall, Margaret: *Bowen Family Systems Theory and Its Uses,* Jason Aronson, New York. A sociologist's perspective.

Kerr, Michael, and Murray Bowen: *Family Evaluation,* W.W. Norton and Co., New York, 1988. Written for therapists but read by many others as well.

Papero, Daniel: *Bowen Family Systems Theory,* Allyn and Bacon, Needham Heights, Mass., 1990. A primer of Bowen family systems theory.

Rosenbaum, Lilian: *Biofeedback Frontiers,* AMS Press, New York, 1989.

Titelman, Peter, editor: *Clinical Applications of Bowen Family Systems Theory,* Haworth Press, New York, 1998.

Toman, Walter: *Family Constellation, Its Effects on Personality and Social Behavior,* Springer Publishing Co., New York, 1961

Appendix 2

A Directory of Psychotherapists Trained in Bowen Family Systems Theory

Fran Ackerman, MSW
Jerusalem, Israel
Phone 011-9722-561-0571
Fax 011-9722-567-0571

Pamela R. Allen, LSCSW
1729 S.W. Oakley
Topeka, Kansas 66604
Phone 913-235-8330
E mail: prallen954@aol.com

Minou T. Arbab, LSCSW, LCSW,
    ACSW
Rockhill Medical Plaza North 6650
Troost, #109
Kansas City, Missouri 64131
Phone 816-361-3830
Fax 816-444-1634

Katharine G. Baker, DSW
Williamsburg, Massachusetts
    01096
Phone 413-268-0111
E mail: BAKERKG@AOL.COM

Sharon Bandstra, LISW
Catholic Social Service
601 Grand Avenue
Des Moines, Iowa 50309
Phone 515-244-3761
Fax 515-237-5070

Mary Catherine Bass, M.Div.,
    MSW, CCSW, ACSW, LMFT
P.O. Box 63
Magnolia, North Carolina
    28453-0063
8404-C Glenwood Ave.
Raleigh, North Carolina 27612

Edward W. Beal, MD
4424 Mongomery Ave., Suite 307
Bethesda, Maryland 20814
Phone 301-656-1699

Beatrice Bennett, LPC
2300 Hickory Crest Drive
Memphis, Tennessee 38138
Phone 901-756-1786

Jean B. Blackburn, MSN, RN, CS
500 South Crest Road
Chattanooga, Tennessee
   37404-0528
Phone and Fax 423-698-8414
E mail: FSTJBB@aol.com

Judith Bohlen, Psy.D.
Bohlen Psychological Services
PO Box 1654
Lenoir, North Carolina 28645
Phone 828-754-0695
Fax 828-754-0695

Clarence Boyd
228 W. Edenton St.
Raleigh, North Carolina 27603
Phone 919-779-3979

Laura Brooks, LCSW-C
810 Light St. Suite 103
Baltimore, Maryland 21330
Phone 410-837-7373

Ann Bunting, Ph.D.
190 Southview Drive
Shelburne, Vermont 05482
Phone 802-863-5536

Betty Carrington, MS, LPC
PO Box 471823
Tulsa OK 74147-1823
Phone 918 742 5155

Polly Caskie, Ph.D.
1675 Riggins Road
Tallahassee, Florida 32306
Phone 850-656-4800,
   800-234-1519
Fax 850-656-4809

Lida Beth Cavanaugh, LICSW
Wareham Area Counseling Service
215 Sandwich Road P.O.Box 31
Wareham, Massachusetts 02571
Phone 508-295-3600
Fax 508-295-4375

Mary Ann Chai, MS, CRNS
Silver Spring, Maryland 20904
Phone 301-847-0909
and
CPC Center
2424 Reedle Drive
Wheaton, Maryland 20902
Phone 301-656-5220

Shirley P. Cloyd, MA
519 Claude Simmons Rd.
Johnson City, Tennessee 37604
Phone 423-282-5064

Patricia A Comella J.D. (Attorney,
   Organizational Consultant)
Georgetown Family Center
4400 MacArthur Blvd., N.W. #103
Washington, D.C. 20007
Phone 202-965-0730
Fax 202-337-6801

David Crum, M.DIV.
1937 S. Mt. Vernon Dr.
Spokane, Washington 99223
Phone 509-533-0270
E mail: decrum@worldnet.att.net

Anne Curran, LCSW
Richmond, Virginia 23229

Vincent DeFrank, LCSW
17053 Road 26
Madera, California 93638
Phone 209-662-1636
Fax 209-662-1637

Josefa R. Delgado, MSW
4840 S.W. Fairlawn Rd.
Topeka, Kansas 66610-2200
Phone 785-862-1857
Fax 785-357-0352

Hal DeShong, Ph.D.
6010 Mt. Bonnell Cove
Austin, Texas 78731-3515
Phone 512-451-9426
Fax 512-371-0147

Des Moines Pastoral
   Counseling Center
550 39th Street
Des Moines, Iowa 50310
Phone 515-274-4006
Fax 515-255-5697

David E. Drake, DO
Dept. of Psychiatry
University of Osteopathic Medicine
   and Health Sciences
3200 Grand Avenue
Des Moines, Iowa 50312
Phone 515-271-1707

Linda Dwyer, MSN, RN, CS
551 Oak Street
Chattanooga, Tennessee 37403
Phone 423-265-2455
Fax 423-265-8336

Gail Feagans, RN, MSN, CS
   (Organizational Consultant)
115 Rosewood Drive
Greenbelt, Maryland 20770-1624
Phone 301-345-1421
E mail: Whalewatchers@juno.com

Patricia Feigley, MSW, LMFT, LISW
1530 Richland Street
Columbia, South Carolina 29201
Phone 803-252-4042
Fax 803-252-7440

Jo Benson Fogel, P.A. (Attorney)
Georgetowne Park
5900 Hubbard Drive
Rockville, Maryland 20852
Phone 301-468-2288
Fax 301-881-9074
E mail: jfogelpa@aol.com

Priscilla J. Friesen, LICSW
Georgetown Family Center
4400 MacArthur Blvd., N.W. #103
Washington, D.C. 20007
Phone 202-965-0730

Randall Frost, M.Div.
384 Newdale Court
North Vancouver, British Columbia, Canada, V7N 3H4
Phone and Fax 604-985-2996
E mail: nfrost@concentric.net

Nancy Galeazzi, LISW
4619 Grand Avenue
Des Moines, Iowa 50312
Phone 515-274-4858

Georgetown Family Center
4400 MacArthur Blvd., N.W. #103
Washington, D.C. 20007
Phone 202-965-0730
Fax 202-337-6801

Roberta M. Gilbert, MD
313 Park Avenue #308
Falls Church, Virginia 22046
Phone 703-532-1501
Fax 703-532-8685

Frances L Giove, LCSW
Georgetown Family Center
4400 MacArthur Blvd. #103
Washington, D.C. 20007
Phone 202-965-0730

Eileen B. Gottlieb, M.Ed., LMFT
Delray Beach, Florida
Phone 561-278-0246
Fax 561-243-6838

Joan S. Grimes, CCSW
Asheville Family Institute
166 E. Chestnut St.
Asheville, North Carolina 28801
Phone 704-254-668

C. Jess Groesbeck, MD
1418 East Blackburn
Mt. Vernon, Washington 98274
Phone 206-424-0440
Fax 916-444-4487
and
1888 Spring Oaks Drive
Springville, Utah 84663
Phone 801-489-8448

C. Margaret Hall, Ph.D.
Sociology Department
Georgetown University
Washington D.C. 20007
Phone 202-687-3983

Victoria Harrison
Family Health Services
7580 Fannin #305
Houston, Texas 77054
Phone 713-790-0226

James E. Hasselle, MD
346 Maine
Lawrence, Kansas 66044
Phone 785-865-2400
Fax 785-865-0014

Laura Havstad, Ph.D.
12651 Fiori Lane
Sebastopol, California 95472
Phone 707-823-1848
Fax 707-823-9374
E mail: HAVSTAD@sonic.net

Tamara J. Hawk, LSCSW
200 Southwind Place #101
Manhattan, Kansas 66503
Phone 785-539-7789
Fax 785-539-8266
E mail: tamihawk@flinthills.com

Carroll Hoskins, MSW
Psychiatric and Family Services of
Greater Kansas City L.L.C.
8340 Mission Road, Suite 201
Prairie Village, Kansas 66206
Phone 913-648-2892
Fax 913-648-6139

Patricia A.S. Hyland, RN, LSCSW
3600 SW Burlingame Rd., Suite 1A
Topeka, Kansas 66611-2097
Phone 785-267-6322

Selden Dunbar Illick, LCSW
Princeton Family Center
14 Vandeventer Ave.
Princeton, New Jersey 08542
Phone 609-683-4188
Fax 609-924-2758

James E. Jones, PH.D.
135 Salina St.
Lafayette, Colorado 80026
Phone 303-666-1131
VM 303-402-0312
Fax 303-441-2902
E-mail: jejones@estreet.com

Joanne G. Kaplan, MSW, LSCSW
121 Whittier
Wichita, Kansas 67207
Phone 316-689-4234
Fax 316-681-0840

Ann G. Karnitschnig, MB, Ch.B.
The Psychotherapy Center
327 West 21st St., Suite 205
Norfolk, Virginia 23517
Phone 757-622-9852
Fax 757-622-4033
and
Behavioral Medicine Inst.
640 Denhight Blvd.
Newport News, Virginia 23608
Phone 757-872-8303
Fax 757-872-6857

Lee Enos Kelley, LCSW
313 Park Ave. #308
Falls Church, Virginia 22046
Phone 703-532-2729

Phil Klever, MSW, LCSW
310 W. 47th St., Suite 215
Kansas City, Missouri 64112
Phone 816-753-7330

Joanna D. Lacoursiere, LSCSW
28 SW Pepper Tree Ln.
Topeka, Kansas 66611
Phone 913-266-0623

Mary Ann Lancaster, RN, CNSC
Richard Hall Community Mental
Health Center
500 North Bridge St.
Bridgewater, New Jersey 08807
Phones 908-253-3166
201-997-7303

Sylvia Landau, MSSW, LCSW
61 South Walnut Bend
Cordova, Tennessee 38018
Phone 901-757-7996
Fax 901-756-9417

Karen Leaman, MSN, RNCS
3671 Robinwood Terrace
Minnetonka, Minnesota 55305
Phone/fax 612-933-1009
E mail: KMLWRG@aol.com

Phil Lorio, MD
Falls Church Virginia

Reen H. Lyddane, MA, LPC
Family Counseling Unit
Juvenile and Domestic Relations
District Court
4000 Chainbridge Road, Rm 2702
Fairfax, Virginia 22030
Phone 703-246-2204

Andrea Maloney-Schara
4400 MacArthur Blvd. #102
Washington, D.C. 20007
Phone 202-965-0730

Joan McElroy, LCSW, CAC
825 Bloomfield Avenue
Verona, New Jersey 07044
and
317 Godwin Avenue
Midland Park, New Jersey 07432
Phone 973-744-3773

Anne McKnight, MSW
Arlington, Virginia

Carole Meredith, MFCC
3703 Camino Del Rio S. #200
San Diego, California 92108
Phone 619-281-6414
Fax 619-281-6380
E mail: Cmeredith1@aol.com

Sally Eisen Miller, Ph.D., LMSW-
ACP,LMFT
6550 Fannin #2339
Houston, Texas 77030
Phone 713-790-0343
Fax 713-668-3897
E mail: Millerdsb@aol.com

Carol Moran, MSW
221 Lawndale Avenue
Wilmette, Illinois 60091-3212
Phone 847-256-0780

M. Joan Munley, Ed.D.
241 East Orange Dr.
Phoenix, Arizona 85012
Phone 602-274-2678
Fax 602-274-2678
E mail: MJLaPaloma@aol.com

Eric C. Nichols, Ph.D.
96 South Union Street
Burlington, Vermont 05401
Phone 802-862-3101
Fax 802-656-3173

Ann V. Nicholson, RN, MS, CS
25A Medway Street
Dorchester Lower Mills,
   Massachusetts 02124
Phone 617-296-4614

Robert J. Noone, Ph.D.
Family Service Center
1167 Wilmette Ave., Ste. 201
Wilmette, Illinois 60091
Phone 847-251-7350
Fax 847-853-2600

Janis Norton, LCSW
420 East Market Street
Harrisonburg, Virginia 22801
Phone 540-433-3727
Fax 540-433-3829
E mail: jnorton@nortoninfo.com

Margaret Otto, LSCSW
3100 N.E. 83rd St., Suite 2350
Kansas City, Missouri 64119
Phone 816-436-1721
Fax 816-436-1180

Robert H. Payne, MD
1620 Ashley River Rd.
Charleston, South Carolina 29407
Phone 803-763-2222
Fax 803-766-5705

Gordon Peterson, MSW, LICSW, CEAP
   (Organizational Consultant)
Workplace Solutions
166 Battery Street
Burlington, Vermont 05401
Phone 802-862-3373
Fax 802-860-4622
E mail: workplaz@together.net

Dolores M. Poole, Ph.D.
4333 S. Dogwood Ave.
Broken Arrow, Oklahoma
74011-1525
Phone 918-451-6355

Sydney Reed, MSW
820 Davis, Suite 221
Evanston, Illinois 60201
Phone 847-866-7357

Lilian Rosenbaum, LCSW-C, Ph.D.
6935 Wisconsin Avenue, Suite 206
Chevy Chase, Maryland 20815
Phone 301-907-9664
Fax 301-340-8958
E mail: lrosenbaum@erols.com

Myra G. Schneider, LCSW
8902 N. Dale Mabry Highway
#211
Tampa, Florida 33614
Phone 813-256-2145
E mail: mschneid@com1.med.-
usf.edu

Mary Sferre, MSW, D.Min.
Mary Steves, MSW, D.Min.
Growth Pointe
3744 Dupont Station Court South
Jacksonville, Florida 32217
Phone 904-731-3261

James B. Smith, MS
Western Pennsylvania Family
Center
733 North Highland Ave.
Pittsburgh, Pennsylvania 15206
Phone 412-421-2415

Walter Howard Smith Jr., Ph.D.
733 North Highland Avenue
Pittsburgh, Pennsylvania 15206
Phone 412-361-1728

Carolyn Harnett Spitz, MSW, CICSW
Lake Geneva, Wisconsin

Eva Sternberg
Hackspettsgatan 4
412 70 Gothenburg Sweden
Phone 46-31-40 33 40
Fax 46-31-40 18 56

Suzanne Stevens, MSW
310 West 47th T. #204
Kansas City, Missouri 64112-1691
Phone 816-531-4922

Michael Sullivan, ACSW,
& Associates
402 S. Union
Traverse City, Michigan 49684
Phone 616-847-0350
Fax 616-947-2138

Ellen Thompson, MSN, RN, CS
R.R. 1 Box 153A
Irasburg, Vermont 05845
Phone 802-754-6868

Peter Titelman, Ph.D.
53 Center Street
Northampton, Massachusetts
  01060
Phone 413-584-7733
Fax 413-586-5942

Bennett Tittler, Ph.D.
Psychiatric Clinic
Melrose Wakefield Hospital
30 Boston Street
Lynn, Massachusetts 01904
Phone 781-593-5110
Fax 781-593-8250

Peggy Treadwell, MSW, LICSW
5420 Grove Street
Chevy Chase, Maryland 20815
Phone 301-654-4126
Fax 301-656-3841

Kent Webb, LCSW
4251 Kipling St., Suite 340
Wheat Ridge, Colorado 90033
Phone 303-420-1362
Fax 303-940-0810

Anthony J. Wilgus, MSW
University of Findlay
  Social Work Program
1000 North Main Street
Findlay, Ohio 45840-3695
Phone 419-422-8313
Fax 419-424-4822
E mail: wilgus@lucy.findlay.edu

Kathy Wiseman, MBA (Organiza-
tional Consultant)
Working Systems, LLC
2000 L Street, Suite 200
Washington, D.C. 20036
Phone 202-659-2222
E mail: Wissuss@aol.com

Index

A

Ackerman, Fran, 128, 136, 160–161, 194
acute anxiety, 72
acute stress
　body's response to, 74–75
ADD, 27
ADHD, 27
adoption, 172–173
　birth parents and, 172
　child focus and, 173
adrenal cortex, 74
adrenal gland, 74
adrenaline, 74, 75
adrenal medulla, 74, 75
Adult Children of Divorce (Beal), 166
alcohol abuse
　violence and, 32
Alcoholics Anonymous, 186
amygdala, 75, 179
anorexia, 43–44
anxiety
　acute, 72
　additive nature of, 72
　brain chemistry and, 37–38
　brain function, 119
　categorizing stressors, 72–73
　chronic, 72, 119–120

defined, 72
displaced to child, 22
effect on body, 23
effects on relationships, 75
as emotional reactivity, 71–72
at higher levels of differentiation, 94
hormone response to, 74
learning problems, 26, 27
physical effect of, 119
in societal regression, 15
from society not family, 29
teenagers, 157–158
thinking ability and, 76
traveling through family, 19–21
traveling through generation, 107–109
anxiety management
　biofeedback, 178–181
　coaching, 177–178
　music and, 183
　play and humor, 177
　talk it out, 181
　thinking it through, 181
　thirty ways to reduce, 182–183
appetite
　stress and, 74

B

babies, 151–152
Baker, Katharine, 136, 162, 170, 189, 193
basic self, 92
  boundary of, 92
  principles and, 92
battle fatigue, 95
Beal, Edward, 166–167, 188
behavior modification, 155
behavior problems
  phases of family relationship, 34–35
  relationship intensity and, 34–35
  symptoms of troubled family relationships, 32
biofeedback, 178–181
birth order. *See* sibling position
boundaries
  of basic self, 92
  benefit of separate, 97
  equality and, 97–98
  of high-level parents, 97, 99
  openness and, 98
  of pseudo or functional self, 92
  relationship fusion, 99–100
  separate boundaries for child-parent relationship, 139–143
  twenty ways to allow child to invade your, 142
  twenty ways to invade your child's, 141
Bowen, Murray, 3–5, 82, 135, 177, 200
Bowen family systems basic concepts
  cutoff, 66

family projection process, 66
multigenerational emotional system, 66
nuclear family emotional system, 65
scale of differentiation of self, 64–65
sibling position, 66
societal emotional process, 66–67
triangles, 64
Bowen family systems theory, 3–5, 57
  advantages of therapy from, 41
  consultation in, 192–193
  emotional process in society, 15–16
  family projection process, 103–106
  multigenerational emotional process, 107–109
  sibling position, 111–114
Bowery Mission, 186
brain chemistry
  anxiety, 37–38
brain disorders, 37
brain function
  anxiety and, 119
  stress and, 74–75
  thinking activity effect on emotion, 76
Bunting, Ann, 36

C

Calhoun, John, 115–116, 118
Califano, Joseph, 13
Campbell, Joseph, 116
Caskie, Polly, 45

child abuse
  marital conflict and, 49
childbirth
  chemical response from body, 74
  as stressor, 74
child focus, 27
  adoption and, 173
  communications in, 89
  displacing anxiety to child by, 22
  effect of worrying on, 81
  emotional illness and, 37, 42
  family projection process,
    104–105
  how specific child becomes, 105
  origin of, 80–81
  parental relationship and, 55, 80,
    82
  parents refocusing steps, 56–57
  physical illness and, 44–45
  in society, 82–83
  as triangle, 82
child/parent relationship, 128
  discipline, 146
  equality in, 143–144
  listening, 146
  open communication, 144–145
  parents defining self, 144–146
  responsibility, 146
  separate boundaries, 139–143
  tips for, 147, 148
children
  parental anxiety displaced in, 22
children, stages of development
  adult offspring, 159–160
  babies, 151–152
  conception and pregnancy,
    150–151

marriage of adult child, 160–161
middle school children, 156–157
school-aged children, 155–156
teenagers, 157–159
toddlers, 152–154
chronic anxiety, 72, 119–120
chronic stress
  body's response to, 74–75
  fight of flight response, 75
  freeze response to, 75
coaching in family systems theory,
  177–178, 191–192
Code Blue, 12
communication
  in child-parent relationship, 144
  divorce, 166–167
  in patterned postures, 89–90
community
  family in, 196
community aids
  for family violence, 51–52
competence, 155
conception, 150
conflict
  behavior examples, 83–85
  communication and, 144
  communication in, 89
  defined, 83
  as response to anxiety, 75
cortisol, 75
cortisone, 74
courts, 14–15
courtship
  chemical response from body, 74
  as stressor, 74
crime
  increase in, 13

prison system working against
family system, 35–36
cults
cutoff and, 34
Curran, Anne, 173
cutoff, 3
concept of, 66
cults and, 34
death of parent and, 169
divorce and, 88, 166
family violence and, 49
gangs and, 34, 87
increasing anxiety from, 87
initial euphoria, 87
as response to anxiety, 75
symptoms of, 87
teen pregnancy and, 33

D
death of parent, 167–169
contact with families of origin,
168–169
deWaal, Franz, 116
discipline, 146, 162
based on principle, 33
distance. *See also* cutoff
behavior example, 85–86
communication and, 89, 144
creating anxiety by, 86
defined, 85
emotional distancing vs. emotional separateness, 86
as response to anxiety, 75
divorce
communication in, 166–167
cutoff and, 88
defined, 165

initial stage of cutoff, 166
level of differentiation of self, 137
rate of, 165
societal regression and, 137
Drake, David, 27
drug use
parents' role in, 13
recovery from, 33
self reports of, 13
by teenagers, 12–13
used to separate from parents,
32–33
violence and, 32
dysfunctional spouse posture. *See*
overfunctioning/underfunction-
ing reciprocity

E
electroencephalographic (EEG)
biofeedback, 180–181
emotional cutoff. *See also* cutoff
defined, 86–87
emotional distancing. *See* distance
emotional illness, 37–42
child focus, 37, 42
emotional maturity, 91
emotional process in society, 15–16
emotional reactivity
benefits of, 71
disadvantages of, 71–72
emotional unit. *See* family as emotional unit
emotions
basing parenting on, 129
focus of therapy, 117
at higher levels of differentiation,
94–95

thinking effect on, 76
equality
   adult offspring and, 160
   sibling position, 143
   in spousal/adult relationship,
      97–98
extended family. *See* family of
   origin; multigenerational
   emotional system
Extraordinary Relationships
   (Gilbert), 5, 200

F
family as emotional unit, 3, 5,
   67–69
   anxiety traveling in, 79–80
   differentiation from, 70
   individuals in, 69
   self defined by, 69
family of origin, 128
   contact with and death of parent,
      168–169
   cutoff and family violence, 49
   grandparents, 193–196
   importance of staying connected
      to, 190–191
family projection process, 66
   child focus and, 105–106
   defined, 104
   example of, 103–104
family systems
   benefit of, 63–64
   difficulty in concept of, 62–64
   one person changes effect on, 61
   vs. individual thinking, 62
   working against corrections
      system, 35–36

family systems theory. *See* Bowen
   family systems theory
family therapy, 2–3
family violence, 47–53
   community aids for, 51–52
   conditions for, 49
   emotional cutoff from families of
      origin, 49
   emotional investment by parents,
      48–49
   extended family connection, 49
   family system approach, 53
   generational patterns of, 50
   kids violent to each other, 49–50
   marital conflict and, 49
   parental approaches for, 50–51,
      53
   steps to calm, 53
feelings. *See* emotions
Felton, Robert, 28
fight or flight response, 75
focused child. *See* child focus
freeze response, 75
Friesen, Priscilla, 179–181
functional self. *See* pseudo or functional self

G
Galea, C., 146
gangs
   cutoff and, 34, 87
Giove, Frank, 18
goals
   of parents, 130–131
Goepfert, Mary, 41
Goodall, Jane, 96, 161
Gottlieb, Eileen, 99, 108–109

grandparents, 193–196
benefits of, 193–194

H
Hall, C. Margaret, 187, 194–196
Harrison, Victoria, 107, 150, 190
hippocampus, 75
Hofer, Myron, 151
holocaust survivors, 108–109
Holt, Roberta, 122
homework, 29
hormones
in stress response, 74–75
Hoskins, Carroll, 172
humor
in families, 176–177
form of play, 175
Hyland, Pat, 51, 162

I
Illick, Selden, 86
immaturity
of parents, 16–17
individual
focus of therapy on, 117
individual thinking
vs. family systems, 62–63
inner guidance system, 99
irresponsibility
society pressure for parents to
accept, 36

K
Kerr, Kathleen, 68, 96, 153
Kuhn, Janet, 169, 186, 194

L
Landers, Ann, 146
Larson, David, 186
latchkey kids, 15
learning problems, 25–30
anxiety and, 26, 27
symptoms of troubled family
relationship and, 32
television and, 154
Lewis, Jerry, 134–135, 177, 196
listening
to children, 146
in higher-functioning families,
98
Lorio, Phil, 134, 146, 176

M
MacLean, Paul, 153, 175
Maloney-Schara, Andrea, 17, 88,
165, 190–191
marijuana
physical effect of, 32
marriage
of adult child, 160–161
McKnight, Anne, 32–33
mental illness, 37
middle school children, 156–157
Morin, Irene, 33
Moyers, Bill, 12
multigenerational emotional
system, 66, 107–109, 128
benefit of researching family
history, 108–109
contact with and death of parent,
168–169
family violence, 49

importance of staying connected
to family of origin, 190–191
Murphy, Douglas, 49
music
anxiety and, 183

N

natural systems, 67–68
neurofeedback, 180–181
nodal events, 73
nuclear family emotional system
concept of, 65

O

oldest children
overfunctioning/underfunction-
ing reciprocity, 88
openness
in higher-functioning families,
98
overfunctioning/underfunctioning
reciprocity
communication and, 144
communication in, 89
defined, 88–89
oldest children, 88
as response to anxiety, 75
overpopulation, 115–116

P

Papero, Dan, 28
parental relationship, 128
child focus and, 80, 82
conflict and child abuse, 49
conflict and family violence, 49
cooperative team, 137
emotional tone of family and,

134
focusing on problem child and,
55
focus on, instead of problem
child, 27–28
importance of, 133
undermining one another, 136
united front, 135–136
parental "we-ness," 101
parenting
basic aspects of, 128
basing on emotions, 129
parenting, high-level
equality, 97–98
inner guidance system, 99
knowledge of self, 99
openness, 98
rebellion and, 98
respect, 98
separate boundaries and, 97, 99
parents. *See also* child-parent
relationship
adoption, 172–173
changing problem focus, 56–57
death of, 167–169
misguided goals of, 131
most important goal for, 130
raising level of differentiation of
self goal, 130
single, 169–170
stepparents and, 170–171
permissiveness, 162–163
popularization of, 16–17
result of, in parenting, 17–18
therapy's role in, 117
personality
sibling position and, 66, 112

physical illness, 43–45
  child focus and, 44–45
  parents' response to, 45
play
  in families, 176–177
  importance in development, 175
pleasure principle
  popularization of, 16–17
  result of, in parenting, 17–18
  therapy's role in, 117–118
pregnancy, 150–151
  rate of teenage, 13–14
principles
  basic self and, 92
  family projection process and,
    106
  at higher levels of differentiation,
    94
  inner guidance system, 99
principles of parents
  discipline based on, 33
  as guide for decisions, 23–24
prison system
  working against family system,
    35–36
problem focus, 27
  displacing anxiety to child by, 22
  moving beyond, 55–57
  parents refocusing steps, 56–57
  physical illness and, 44–45
pseudo or functional self, 92–93
  boundary of, 92
psychotherapy
  disadvantages of, 41

R

relationship fusion
  boundaries and, 99–100
  at higher levels of differentiation,
    93, 94
  at lower levels of differentiation,
    93, 101
  at mid-levels of differentiation,
    93
  parental "we-ness," 101
relationships. *See also* child-parent
    relationship; parental relation
    ship
  communication types and
    patterns of, 89–90
  importance of understanding, 2,
    3
  as most important parent goal,
    130
  needs for, in children, 128
  as source of anxiety, 75–76
respect
  in higher-functioning families,
    98
responsibility, 156
  to children, 146
  encouraging, 36
responsible I, 101–102
Ritalin, 27
Rosemond, John, 154
Rosenbaum, Lilian, 75, 179

S

scale of differentiation of self
  basic self, 92
  boundaries and, 97
  changes in, over lifetime, 91

compared to emotional maturity, 91

concept of, 64–65

divorce and, 137

at higher levels of differentiation, 94–95

high-level parents, 97–102

at lower levels of differentiation, 93–96

measurement of, 92

pseudo or functional self, 92–93

raising level of, as parental goal, 130

vs. selfishness, 101–102

school-aged children, 155–156

schools

family relationships repeated at, 26–27

homework, 29

role of, 14

safety and, 28–29

societal regression and, 28–30

self

basic, 92

defined in terms of relationship, 69

knowledge of, and parenting, 99

pseudo or functional, 92–93

self-confidence, 155

selfishness

vs. scale of differentiation of self, 101–102

sexual activity

rate for teenagers, 13

shock wave effect, 73

sibling position, 66, 111–114

combinations for, 112

equality and, 143

finding strengths in, 113

personality and, 112

unique characteristics from, 70

siblings, 128

family projection process and, 66, 103–106

play and, 175

single parents, 14, 169–170

sleep

stress and, 74

Smith, Tessa, 75

Smith, Walter Howard, 48

Sobel, Bonnie, 76–77

societal emotional process

concept of, 66–67

societal regression

causes of, 16

concept of, 66–67

defined, 15

divorce and, 137

family role in, 118

nuclear family in, 121–123

overpopulation and, 115–116

pressure on families toward regressive decisions, 23

problem focus and, 55–56

providing opportunities for vulnerable children, 23

role of therapy in shaping regression, 116–119

schools and, 28–30

signs of, 12

symptoms of, 115

triggers for, 67, 115–116

violence and, 50

Soviet Union, 115, 193–194

spirituality, 185–188
stepparents, 170–171
stress
  fight of flight response, 75
  freeze response to, 75
  management tools for, 76–77
  ovulation and, 150
  pregnancy and, 151
stressors
  categorizing, 72–73
  chemical response in body from,
    74
  nodal events, 72
  optimal stress and body response,
    74
  shock wave effect, 73
substance abuse. See drug use
suicide
  teenage, 14
Sullivan, Michael, 34–35, 183
symptomatic child. See child focus
systems
  defined, 67
  natural, 67–68

T
Tannen, Deborah, 153
teenagers, 157–159
  anxiety in family unit and,
    157–158
  crime by, 13
  drug use by, 12–13
  pregnancy, 13–14, 33
  sexual activity of, 13
  as stormy periods, 158, 159
  suicide, 14

tips to enhance relationships
  with, 159
television
  isolation and, 12
  learning disabilities, 154
theory
  benefit of, 63–64
  difficulty in concept of, 61–62
therapy
  from Bowen theory, 41
  family, 2–3
  patient-focused, 44–45
  psychotherapy, 41
  role of, in shaping societal
    regression, 116–119
thinking
  effect on emotional part of brain,
    76
  at higher levels of differentiation,
    94–95
toddlers, 152–154
Toman, Walter, 66, 111, 112, 200
Treadwell, Peggy, 185–186
triangles
  biofeedback and, 180
  child focus as, 82
  concept of, 64
  as response to anxiety, 75
  stepparents and, 170
  united front and, 136

U
Udry, Richard, 158
underfunctioning. See overfunc-
  tioning/underfunctioning reciprocity
united front, 135–136

V

violence. *See also* family violence
   drug abuse, 32
   schools and, 28–29
   societal regression, 50

W

witch hunts, 122–123
worrying about child
   changing worried focus to self, 82
   effect of, 81
   increasing child's anxiety, 29

Y

Yankelovich, Daniel, 118

Z

Zigler, Edward, 14